MW00658315

THE 1931 HASTINGS BANK JOB & THE BLOODY BANDIT TRAIL

Monty McCord

THE History PRESS

Published by The History Press
Charleston, SC 29403
www.historypress.net

First published 2013

Manufactured in the United States

ISBN 978.1.60949.796.5

Library of Congress CIP data applied for.

Notice: The information in this book is true and complete to the best of our knowledge. It is offered without guarantee on the part of the author or The History Press. The author and The History Press disclaim all liability in connection with the use of this book.

For Ann…the one.

Contents

Preface

I learned of the 1931 Hastings bank robbery in the 1970s while working on my first book, a history of the Hastings police department. After stints at the Adams and Phelps County sheriff's offices, I joined the HPD in 1978. The book was locally printed four years later. Over the next thirty years, between other book projects, I saved bits of information about the robbery for a possible article. But the more I learned about it, the more I wanted to know.

Working with many different sources, particularly newspapers across the country, it isn't always easy to glean the actual story. In fact, the various aspects of this book took a bit of detective work to decipher. It was necessary to recognize reporters' errors so they didn't derogate the story. After many years of study, I'm confident that the facts have finally revealed themselves.

I decided that, considering such a momentous crime, I was looking at only half of the story. I wanted to know who the bank bandits were and where they came from. Had they robbed any other banks? What became of them after they left Hastings with "our" money?

The facts of the bank robbery itself were well covered by local newspapers, but the mystery remained. What happened to the bandits afterward? Research over time would reveal the mystery…or would it?

Acknowledgements

I am truly grateful to the many wonderful people who helped in one way or another with this work. I list them here in no particular order and with the sincere hope that I haven't forgotten anyone.

I would like to begin by offering a very special thank you to Darran Fowler, publisher, and Don Seaton, owner of the *Hastings Tribune*, whose complete support and willingness to share materials helped to make this book complete. The *Tribune*'s detailed coverage of the bank robbery allowed for a nearly step-by-step narrative.

A sincere thank you to my wife, Ann, for all of her help—research, editorial, technical—but most importantly, for her support of my work.

Also a thank you to Mark Schreiber, deputy warden (retired) of Missouri Department of Corrections, who shared his time and historical knowledge of the old prison, and to Ray Miller, a volunteer prison tour guide (www.missouripentours.com), both friends worth having. My appreciation also goes to Jon Bruning, Nebraska attorney general; Sonya Fauver, Nebraska Board of Pardons; Richard Witt, Catherine Renschler, Carol Kleppinger and Karen Butler of the Adams County Nebraska Historical Society; Patricia Freeman, Webb City, Missouri Genealogical Society; Linda Williams, clerk of the Circuit Court, Carthage, Missouri; Jeanne Babb, Jasper County Missouri Circuit Court; Andy Howell, *Ogden Standard-Examiner*; Jeannene Douglass, Nebraska Department of Correctional Services; Gayla Koerting, Linda Hein and Matt Piersol from the Nebraska State Historical Society; Christy Smith, Texas Ranger Hall of Fame and Museum; Jeanne Newby and Peggy

Duty, Central Texas Genealogical Society; Cathy Spitzenberger, University of Texas at Arlington Library; Matt Swearengin, *Durant Daily Democrat*; Zoe Ann Stoltz, Montana Historical Society; KC May Sackman, Montana Old Prison Museum; Ken Fisk, the Coin Center; Linda Merryman, Waco-McLennan County Texas Library; Susan Wentroth and Beverly Mossman, Oklahoma Historical Society; Jackie Williamson and Annette Laber, Thayer County Museum; Herman Kirkwood, Oklahoma Outlaw-Lawman History Association; Oklahoma State Department of Health; Sergio Valasco, Texas State Library and Archives Commission; George Goldthwaite; Gail Hughes; Dolores Lindsay; Ron Lukesh; Lenn and Lauretta Woods; Cyndi Snokhous; Martha Williams; Randal Chick; Carl Montgomery; Charlie Vogel; Tommy Dryden; Ray Thomas; Deborah Hatten Lacey; Leon Davis; Floyd Marian; and Pat Toscano.

Introduction

This is the story of the Hastings National Bank robbery of 1931 and the trail of blood spread by the Texas and Oklahoma bandits who perpetrated the crime, a trail that stretched into the 1950s. But first, a little background is in order.

The state of Nebraska did not escape the rash of bank robberies that plagued the Midwest during the Roaring Twenties and Dirty Thirties. Nor, as history shows us, did the robberies begin during those times. Citizens often read newspaper accounts of these and other crimes throughout the state before the 1920s.

One such article appeared prior to the Hastings bank robbery, fourteen years to the day, in fact, detailing Nebraska lawman Jim Malone's battle with bank robbers in the early years of the twentieth century. In part it said, "The history of Nebraska bank robberies sounds like a chapter from a Diamond Dick magazine. It deals with 'bad men,' sure enough detectives, and a gang so organized and controlled by a few leading spirits that for years Nebraska bankers labored under the danger of robberies more apparent and more real than any other state in the nation."

On May 1, 1917, prohibition went into effect in Nebraska (two years before national prohibition), and with it came new responsibilities for the governor. State law made it the duty of the governor to enforce the prohibition law and a law against the theft of automobiles and gave him the power to employ whatever assistants he needed to carry out enforcement. Shortly before the law went into effect, Governor Neville explained, "The enforcement of the new law rests upon the local authorities and they will be held to strict accountability for the failure to enforce same." The governor's appointee for the job was called "chief deputy law enforcement officer." The chief's assistants were called "state agents" of the law enforcement department (or division). They were commonly referred to as the "state sheriff" and "deputy state sheriffs." It was also the duty of the state sheriff to assist local law enforcement agencies, when requested, with any crimes that were above their ability to manage. This most often involved major crimes, including bank robberies, at a time when offenders were highly mobile and could flee through several counties and even cross state lines to make good their escape.

One major case culminated in September 1927. Richard Brumfield and Lester and Donald Barge were arrested in Minot, North Dakota, in response to circulars sent out by Nebraska state sheriff William C. Condit. (The office of state sheriff had officially been created that year, even though the title had been in use for several years.) Brumfield and Barge had stolen a car in San Francisco and driven to Nebraska, where their crime spree continued. They were wanted for robberies and attempted robberies of banks at Hamlet, Saronville, Taylor and Smithfield in Nebraska and Hillrose, Colorado. During the attempted robbery of the Taylor bank, the sheriff was kidnapped and the town marshal wounded. They were also wanted for the murders of a bank cashier in North Dakota and a marshal in Minnesota.

In 1930, when Nebraska banks lost $200,000 from six bank robberies within a week's time, state American Legion officers were prompted to ask for the formation of Legion vigilante committees. The department commander proposed that veterans, having been battle tested in France during the World War, be armed with rifles, machine guns, ammunition and fast cars "to be ready for action at strategic points." In part, the Legion commander explained, "If the present epidemic of bank robberies continues, insurance rates would increase so as to become practically prohibitive...It will mean that law and order will break down; that our money and our property will not be safe in our homes."

Procedures to be followed included cooperation of local telephone companies, which would call out posse members by phone; deciding on predetermined points at which roadblocks would be set up; establishing techniques for marking routes taken while chasing bandits; and dissemination of information regarding descriptions of robbers and their vehicles.

Approval of the American Legion plan by State Sheriff Condit and State Attorney General C.A. Sorensen surely illustrated the high level of frustration with the crime wave. The Lincoln National Bank in the state's capital city was robbed of $2.5 million only days before this newspaper article appeared. This was one of the largest robberies in the country at a time when bandits routinely escaped with a few thousand dollars.

The protective committee of the Nebraska Bankers Association recommended a stringent program for preventing bank robberies that included alarms, trained guards and guidelines for police, telephone offices and other authorities in case of a robbery. The most drastic part of the suggested program was establishing a $1,000 reward for killed or captured bandits. By March 1931, after many more robberies, the association reported that most banks had approved the "dead bandit fund," but not enough had submitted monies for the establishment of a standing fund. Other states were looking at rewards of this type as well.

Members of the bankers association were not the only folks concerned about the plague of bank robberies. State representative George R. Curry of Arapahoe declared that he would introduce a bill providing for capital punishment for bank robbery. "I actually believe that bank robberies that place victims in fear of their lives are more serious and menacing to public welfare than ordinary murder, and that they deserve equal punishment," Mr. Curry said.

Located in south central Nebraska, the city of Hastings, in Adams County, had a population of around fifteen thousand in 1931. Primarily an agricultural area, Hastings was also home to many businesses that were starting to feel the strain of the national economic depression that began with the stock market collapse of 1929. The old city jail, attached to the rear of the fire station, was remodeled to handle the growing number of transients moving through Hastings. Six banks served the town during the 1920s, but by 1931, only three banks remained. They appeared to be doing well.

The January 17, 1931 edition of the *Hastings Daily Tribune* ran an article on the health of those remaining banks. To the criminal mind, it must have read like an invitation. The article began with the eye-opening statement, "With almost $5,000,000 on deposit in Hastings banks at the close of 1930, financial conditions in the Hastings trade territory were reflected as being unusually favorable here." The figure represented only a 5 percent decrease since 1929, which was explained by a surplus of crops. Instead of selling at low prices, farmers were holding onto their grain, thus reducing bank deposits. The year 1930 was reported to have been a profitable one for each of the three Hastings banks. The article wraps up this way, "At all times during 1930, as well as at the present time, there was and is a bountiful supply of money on hand here—a supply sufficient in amount to well take care of the needs of any legitimate enterprise." It's unknown if any of the bandits who came to Hastings saw the article, but if they had, it surely would have caught their attention!

The first bank robbery in Adams County was carried out on October 18, 1906, in the village of Pauline, ten miles south of Hastings. Robbers blew the safe of the Bank of Pauline, which was connected to the First National Bank of Hastings, and got away with $1,500.

The second bank robbery, the subject of this book, occurred on February 25, 1931, when the Hastings National Bank was robbed of over $27,000. It was called "the slickest job that has been pulled on a Nebraska bank in history," by William B. Hughes Jr., secretary of the Nebraska Bankers Association. The following day, the Hastings robbery even made the *New York Times* with a headline, "BANK ROBBERS SHOOT WAY THROUGH POSSE—Wound Officer and Escape Trap After $27,173 Theft at Hastings, Neb." The article continued on with information about "THREE OTHER BIG HOLD-UPS" (on February 25, 1931, date of the Hastings robbery), which were the $26,000 robbery of a branch of the Whitney Bank and Trust Company in New Orleans, Louisiana; the $20,000 robbery of the Union Trust Company in Dayton, Ohio; and the $12,000 robbery of the Bank of Burlington in Burlington, Wisconsin. The take at Hastings was actually $27,673, plus a $100 diamond ring, bringing the total to $27,773, more than any of the other three robberies covered that day.

Part I

CHAPTER 1
Bank Job

There is a bountiful supply of money on hand here.
—Hastings Daily Tribune, *January 17, 1931*

"As free from crime as any city in Nebraska is the record the Hastings Police Department compiled for Hastings during the year 1930," a *Tribune* article declared. It reported on the department's annual activity, which included 416 arrests, helping to make "a splendid record during the past year." Police news for 1930 included a move from their second-story rooms at First Street and Hastings Avenue to a new headquarters building that adjoined the fire and street departments at First and Burlington Avenue.

The police department consisted of: Chief John Bramble; Captain Frank Yetman; day desk sergeant Elbert A. Dailey; day patrolmen William O'Brien, Ben Scheele, James L. Wood, Thomas Dryden and Melvin McGuire; night desk sergeant Ray Thomas; and night patrolmen Lowell Wooding and Neil Wheat. In May 1930, the city council appointed Caroline Wahlquist policewoman at a salary of fifty dollars per month. Half of her salary was paid by the local Red Cross, and she was posted there. "Welfare work and police work are so closely aligned it is rather difficult at times, to say just where one begins and the other ends," Wahlquist said.

The city also purchased two new Ford Model A roadsters, painted green with black fenders, for use as police cars. The doors were lettered in gold, "Police Patrol—No. 1 (&2) Hastings, Nebr."

In late February 1931, local clothier Wolbach and Brach ran ads announcing its upcoming "Sensational Selling Event," where dresses would be on sale for $8.88. The Ford dealer offered new cars from $430.00 to $630.00, and D.W. Griffith's *Lincoln* was showing at the Strand Theatre. The Rivoli Theatre, located across the intersection from the Hastings National Bank at Second Street and Denver Avenue, was showing Edna Ferber's *Cimarron*. The film starred Richard Dix and Irene Dunn and was described in the newspaper as "exploding the confines of the printed page in a flame-shot shower of tumultuous emotion."

Citizens of Hastings would soon experience some exploding and tumultuous emotion for real during an event that would be talked about for years. National newspaper coverage of the event would bring a certain amount of notoriety to the south central Nebraska town.

Shortly after 6:00 a.m. on February 25, 1931, a man identified only as Cox walked past a new, black Chevrolet sedan parked along the east side of the Hastings National Bank. His immediate goal in the morning darkness was to check the thermometer that was mounted on the east side of the bank. The weather was mild for February in Nebraska, with early temperatures in the mid-thirties and afternoon highs near fifty degrees. In fact, it reportedly was the warmest winter in fifty years. Directly across Denver Avenue was the Stone Block building, so-called because of its sandstone block construction. Across the street to the southeast was the McClelland-Dunn Motor Company, the local Ford dealer. When Cox stopped momentarily and struck a match to read the thermometer, he noticed a man step out of the Chevrolet. Cox didn't think much about it at the time, noting that the man got back inside the car as he walked away. Little did he know that at about 4:00 a.m., three men had jimmied a rear side window of the very bank he was standing next to and gained entry.

At about 6:20, William Meininger approached the front door of the bank where he worked as janitor. One of his first responsibilities on winter mornings was to fire up the furnace so the bank would be a comfortable temperature when employees started to arrive. As the janitor stepped inside and closed the door, two men took hold of him. He grabbed one of his attackers by the throat and started yelling. One of the men told him, "Look here, you, if you don't keep still, we'll kill you!" Meininger saw the guns held by the men and wisely cooperated, saying, "I'll keep still, I'm too old a man to make noises. I like to live a while longer."

The three bandits that Meininger saw in the bank wore masks. After binding his hands with wire, they asked Meininger several questions.

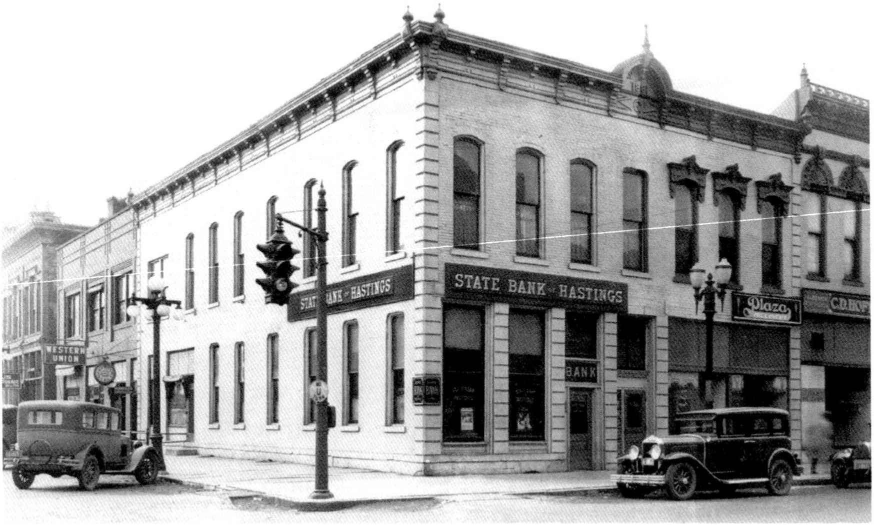

Shortly before the robbery, the State Bank of Hastings had been sold, and the new Hastings National Bank signs had yet to be placed. This is how the bank appeared at the time of the robbery. *Courtesy of the Adams County Historical Society.*

Anxious to know if the bank had an alarm system, the bandits asked what various items in the bank were for and how many employees worked there. They wanted to know who the cashier was and who could open the vault, and noted the descriptions of each. They asked if the female employees were married and were told by the janitor, "No, they were all single." They also asked when the sign painter would arrive, which was proof that they had indeed followed the protocol of bank robbers in "casing" their target. Just the month before, the bank had changed hands from the State Bank of Hastings to the Hastings National Bank. A local sign painter had recently been contracted to paint new signs on the doors and windows of the bank, and only through prior surveillance would the bandits have been aware of this.

Meininger was asked for instructions on how to fire up the furnace. One of the bandits started the furnace, telling Meininger that he didn't want the bank employees to be cold when they came in. They then moved the janitor to the women's basement toilet room. As he sat down there, he could distinctly hear a car start up and drive away about every five minutes, first from the east side of the bank and then from the front. He could tell by the sound that it was the same car. Meininger later explained to reporters,

"They seemed to move the car about every five minutes. After they had taken the money, I heard the car drive away and then heard no more of it."

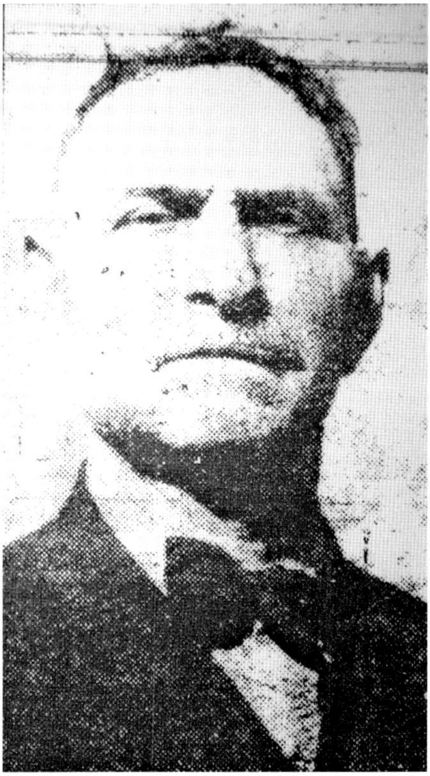

William Meininger, the bank janitor, was the first to be taken hostage by awaiting bandits when he arrived for work. *Courtesy of the* Hastings Tribune.

Over the next two and a half hours, thirteen bank officers and employees came to work, were met at the door by the bandits and then escorted to the basement, where they were bound with wire. Sign painter Frank Lindsay made fourteen. The group included bank president Howard Pratt; vice-president O.A. Riley; Herbert E. Nelson, Ivan Riley, Charles Deets, Leo Swigle, Joseph Bauer, Orville Greenfield, Francis Weiler, Clinton Norris, Dorothy Park, Hazel Horn, William Meininger and Lindsay. The bandits bound their prisoners' hands and feet with wire that they brought with them specifically for that purpose. The men were gagged with cloth that was tied around their heads and through their mouths and then secured with wire. The wire left deep red marks on their faces, which were still evident hours later. They were forced to lie on the floor while the women were allowed to sit in chairs. The gags used on the women were held in place with rubber bands.

About 7:30, Hastings postman Henry Holt knocked at the rear door of the bank to make his daily delivery. When no one came to the door, he "kicked it several times—hard enough to attract the attention of anyone that might be inside." The door was partly opened by a man about five feet ten inches tall, wearing a gray coat and cap. He did not wear a mask. Holt handed over a parcel post package and then went on his way. He later reported, "I had delivered packages to the bank at that hour before. I had never seen this man. At the time however, I thought he was a new employee."

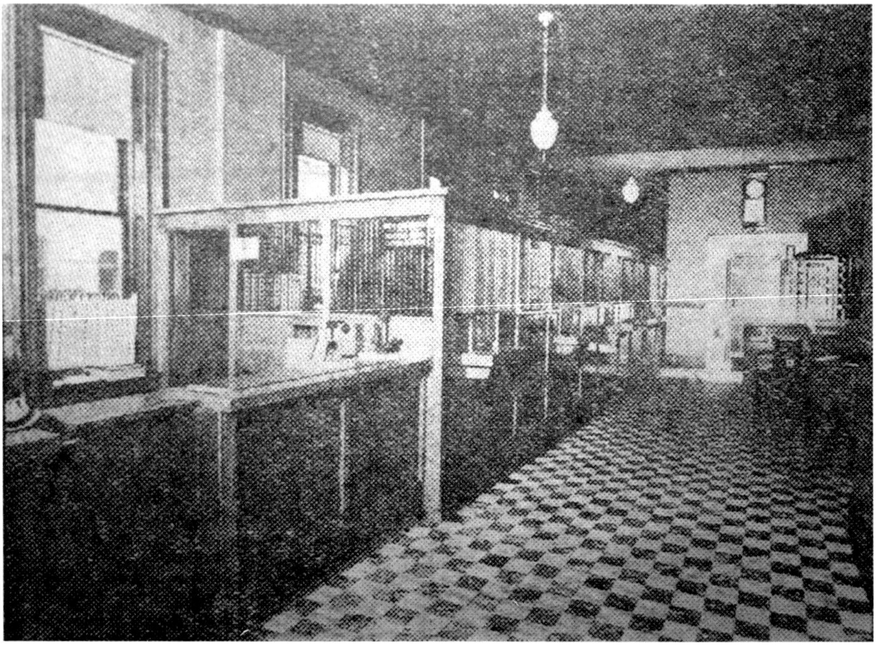

Lobby of the Hastings National Bank. As employees arrived, they were taken to the back stairway and to the basement where they were confined. *Courtesy of the* Hastings Tribune.

Only Meininger and Dorothy Park offered the bandits any challenge. When Miss Park arrived and was escorted toward the stairs, she broke away and ran the length of the lobby screaming. One of the bandits caught her before she got to the front door and took her to the basement.

O.A. Riley, cashier of the bank, arrived about 8:20. When he entered the bank, two bandits told him to go on downstairs with the rest. The same was done with bank president Howard Pratt when he arrived. Pratt was later quoted as saying, "The fellow who was watching the others in the storeroom (in the basement) didn't hear me come down, and I had a minute of fear that he might turn around quickly and shoot me thinking I was coming to get him."

Assistant cashier Herbert Nelson was brought upstairs to wait until the vault's time lock released at 8:30. When it did, he was told to unlock the huge vault door. He asked, "Is this a command?" The firm reply came quickly, "You bet your life it is."

While the third masked bandit, described as being "tall and dark," busied himself with emptying the vault, Nelson was returned to the basement where he was tied up. He soon remembered that he had forgotten to unlock the box containing the gold reserve supply and thought it better to tell the bandits before they discovered it themselves. He was escorted back upstairs to the vault, where he unlocked the gold and then was returned to the basement.

Less than ten minutes later, the three bandits walked out of the bank by way of a basement door that led to the street, got inside their waiting car and were driven away. They left with $22,943 in currency, $1,800 in gold, $2,930 in silver and a $100 diamond ring, for a grand total of $27,773. Their take was equivalent to approximately $425,000 in today's dollars. A large quantity of negotiable securities was left untouched. Items like that required a reliable "fence" who could sell them to special markets.

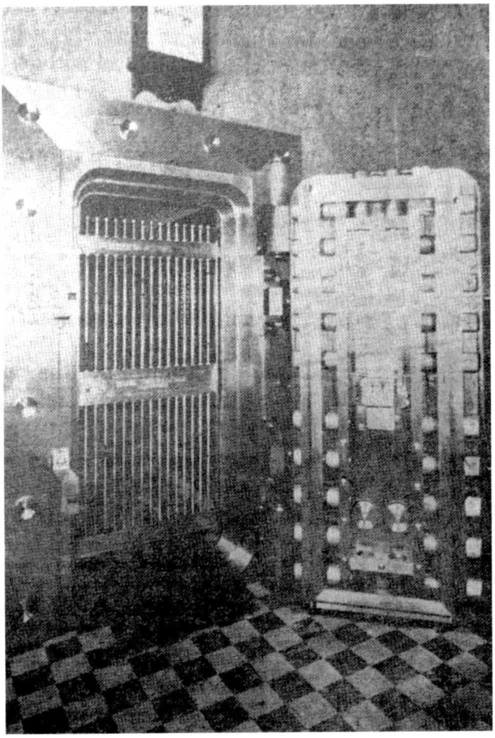

The bank vault was equipped with a substantial state-of-the-art door that operated on a time lock. *Courtesy of the* Hastings Tribune.

Marguerite Bierman, a teller for the bank, arrived within minutes of the bandits' departure. Surprised that no one was in the bank when she walked in, she first thought that the others had played a joke on her. When she heard their voices in the basement, she went down and found them bound with wire. After she untied her fellow employees, the alarm was sounded.

On the morning of the robbery, motorcycle officer Tommy Dryden made a routine stop at a gas station at Twelfth Street and Kansas Avenue to phone headquarters. Two-way police radios were several years away at this time, and officers were required to check in periodically by telephone to see if they had any calls. Dryden was notified of the bank robbery and instructed to return to the station.

The employees related their experiences to Hastings police and included descriptions of the bandits. The apparent leader was described as large of build, probably six feet two inches in height, weighing from 180 to 200 pounds and wearing a light gray topcoat and cap. Another of the gang was

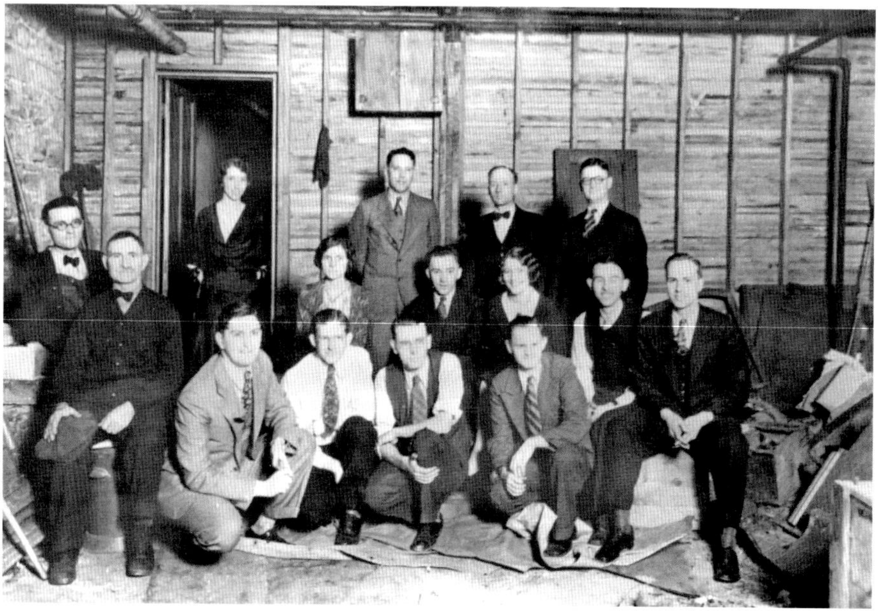

Employees of the Hastings National Bank pose for a newspaper photographer in the basement where they were tied up and gagged. *Back row:* Howard Pratt, Herbert Nelson, O.A. Riley. *Seated center:* Hazel Horn, Joe Bauer, Dorothy Park, Leo Swigle, Charles Deets. *Kneeling, front row:* Ivan Riley, Clinton Norris, Orville Greenfield, Francis Weiler. *Far left:* (In glasses) sign painter Frank Lindsay and William Meininger. Marguerite Bierman (standing in doorway) arrived only minutes after the bandits fled and helped to free fellow employees. *Courtesy of the* Hastings Tribune.

described as small in stature, about five feet four inches tall, wearing a light-colored suit. A third bandit was described as being about five feet seven inches tall, about thirty years old and speaking with a distinct southern accent. The fourth bandit was described as being about thirty years old, with sandy hair combed straight back and wearing a gray suit. There may have been some confusion about the fourth bandit, as it was determined that only three were in the bank. Other informants made it clear, however, that the fourth bandit stayed with the car outside the bank. It was common practice to leave a man outside, not only to serve as a lookout to warn the others if police arrived but to be the getaway driver as well. It was reported that the bandits left in a new Chevrolet sedan (the same one Mr. Cox saw as he checked the bank's thermometer) bearing Lancaster County, Nebraska license plates.

Hazel Horn said the next day, "It was a circus. I wouldn't have missed it for the world. And, we must admit that the bandits were very polite—especially to the ladies. One of them, especially, was very considerate. I

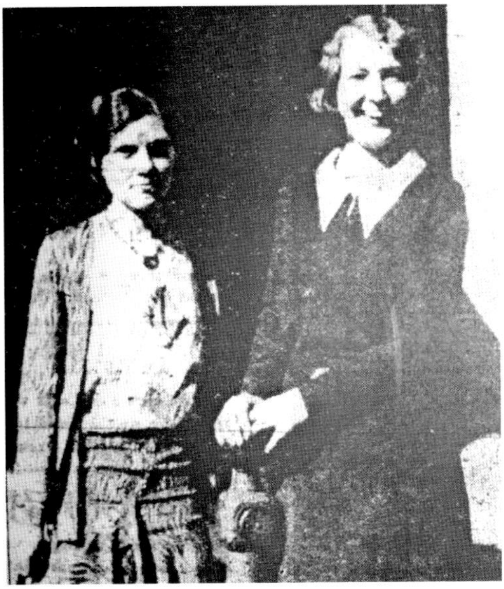

Bank employees Hazel Horn (left) and Dorothy Park. As Park was being escorted to the bank basement, she broke away from the bandit's grasp and ran screaming through the lobby until she was recaptured. *Courtesy of the* Hastings Tribune.

remember that he told me he would loosen the binding on my hands if it was hurting me, and even apologized for mussing my hair a bit when he placed a blindfold over my head." She added, "I think he was pretty nice."

Dorothy Park, the employee who momentarily broke loose from the grip of the bandits and ran screaming through the bank, said, "I hope we don't have to go through that experience again, but if we do, I don't think I'll make a sound next time." Marguerite Bierman was visibly disappointed in missing the event. She lamented, "I would miss out on the only bank holdup they ever had in Hastings. If I had known that someone was waiting for me, I think I would have hurried more, even though it were a bandit." The somewhat misguided attitudes of these young women weren't all that uncommon at the time due to the perceived notion that these Depression-era gangsters led a romantic and exciting life, albeit usually a short one.

A more sensible view was given by bank president Howard Pratt. He said, "I'll confess that I was really scared." He was on his own momentarily when sent to the basement. He explained, "There was a telephone near at hand and I considered using it to call police—but only for a minute. I decided if I did they would plug me, and that's probably what they would have done."

The bankers association believed that up to that time, no other bank robbery in Nebraska had been executed with such a degree of pre-planning and using the technique of breaking into the bank hours before opening and capturing each employee as they arrived for work. The following day, the bank ran a large ad in the newspaper that reported its $500,000 burglary insurance and assured customers of no loss through robbery. When the bank reopened, the lobby became packed with curiosity seekers, but no one made any requests to withdraw their money.

CHAPTER 2

Hide-Out, Shootout and Hostages

Don't kill him in cold blood. Give him a chance.
—Officer Wood, as reported in the Hastings Daily Tribune, *May 5, 1931*

By nine o'clock that tense morning of February 25, officials of the Lincoln Telephone and Telegraph Company in Hastings reported that telephone wires were handling the largest load since the signing of the Armistice in 1918. Hastings police chief John Bramble soon added to that load after interviewing bank employees and collecting various reports from the public. With help from the state sheriff's office, he notified law enforcement agencies throughout Nebraska and northern Kansas of the bandits' descriptions and asked them to be on the lookout. Radio stations KMMJ in Clay Center and KFAB in Lincoln also broadcast descriptions of the hold-up men.

The suspect descriptions given by bank employees were not complete nor very accurate, which is not unusual, especially from people under stress. The *Hastings Democrat* noted, "One (suspect) is said to have displayed a couple of gold teeth in front and looked like a foreigner. All wore light top coats. But no two descriptions agree in the main details."

A crowd of people gathered at police headquarters. Onlookers watched and waited for developments and helped to spread the growing flood of rumors that occupied them throughout the day.

The police were inundated with reports of suspicious cars and people. Officers did their best to check out as many of these reports as possible, stopping many people unknown to them, only to release them after their identification checked out. One report was given some credence. Harry Marian, who lived at 1918 West Third Street, reported to Chief Bramble that at about the time the bandits were said to have made their escape, he saw a dark-colored sedan speeding north on Lincoln Avenue in the downtown area. He said the car turned west on Third Street and failed to stop for traffic signals. Marian added that a number of men were in the car—four, he thought.

Meanwhile, Volcott Condit, a special officer for the Nebraska Bankers Association, was sent from Lincoln to Hastings. Also from Lincoln, State Sheriff Michael Endres dispatched deputies Fred Benton and Eugene Batton, though their involvement in the Hastings bank robbery was minimal, as Chief Bramble headed the investigation.

Notification of Adams County sheriff Raymond Crosson was inadvertently overlooked in the commotion, but he quickly learned of the robbery from the state sheriff's office. Crosson then joined in to assist Chief Bramble with the case.

A *Hastings Daily Tribune EXTRA* hit the streets shortly after ten o'clock that

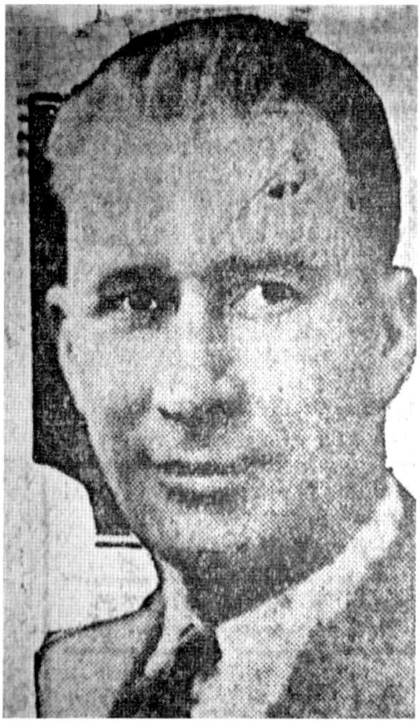

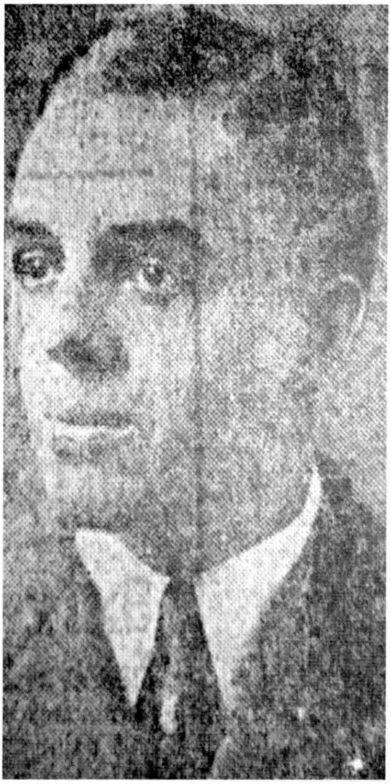

Top: Hastings police chief John Bramble led the bank robbery investigation. *Courtesy of the* Hastings Tribune.

Right: Nebraska Bankers Association special officer Volcott Condit was wounded in the shootout with the bandits at their house on East Sixth Street. *Courtesy of the* Hastings Tribune.

morning. Nearly one thousand copies were sold in an hour. The regular noon edition, which included up-to-the-minute details of the robbery, sold almost as well as the extra.

An article in that day's *Tribune* included information given by Earl Hunter of H.E. Bowman and Company, a real estate and insurance business located at 123 North Denver Avenue. The business adjoined the rear of the Hastings National Bank building. Hunter explained that on the Friday before the robbery, a man came into the office and said he was interested in buying some land. He didn't seem to care "whether the land was one mile or ten from the city or whether its price was $100 or $175 an acre." The man stepped to the north wall and roused the suspicions of the employees when he seemed more interested in looking at the north wall than the maps. (The north wall of the Bowman company office was the south wall of the bank vault). The employees remembered that the man's right coat pocket looked weighted down and speculated that cash or a pistol was inside. They also noticed that the man's fingers were blackened as though he had handled something greasy. He was described as being of medium height, with light, well-groomed hair, wearing a dark suit without a hat.

The man's close scrutiny of the wall was immediately reported to Police Chief Bramble and Ivan Riley at the bank. Some people said after the robbery that they had seen a man fitting this description walking back and forth along the east side of the bank during the early morning hours.

By evening, the crowd in front of the police station had dissipated, but the robbery was still the main topic of conversation around town. At this point in time, there was no doubt much conjecture as to the robbers' location. Officers continued to watch for any suspicious types, but the general belief was that the bank robbers were long gone.

Chief Bramble sat in his office and pored through the myriad of reports that had been received that day as Mayor Joe Davis looked on. Three of the reports regarded a house at 810 East Sixth Street, on the east edge of town. The occupants of the house had been under suspicion for a couple weeks as possible bootleggers. Bramble recalled that the first report about that property had been filed a month previously by Arthur Lawson. Mr. Lawson had rented the house to a Mr. and Mrs. Robert Hendricks the last week of January. Hendricks had told Lawson that he traveled for a drug company and that he and his wife would move in the following week. Lawson had decided to check over the house to see that everything was in order before Hendricks moved in on the twenty-ninth. At that time, he found a couple suits and some bedding in the supposedly empty house, as if someone had

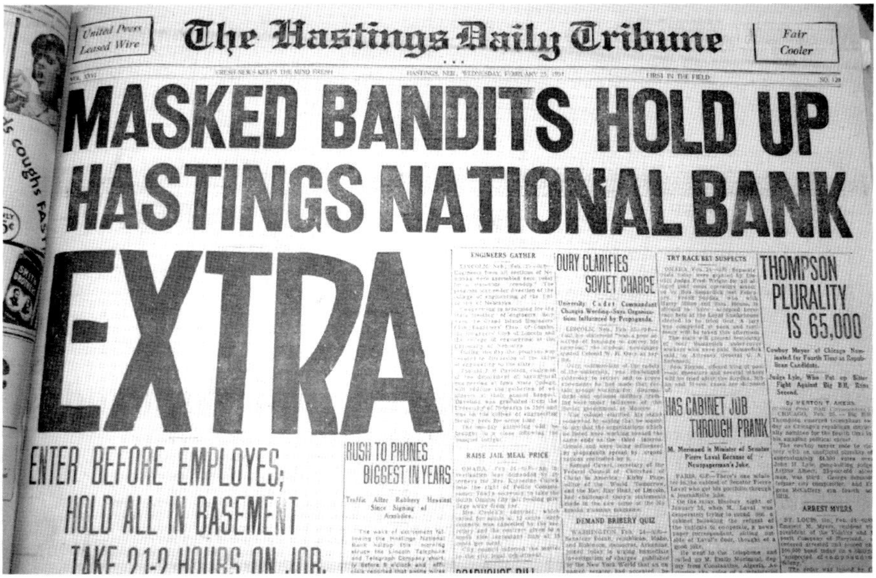

The Hastings Daily Tribune

United Press Leased Wire

Fair Cooler

MASKED BANDITS HOLD UP HASTINGS NATIONAL BANK

EXTRA

ENTER BEFORE EMPLOYES; HOLD ALL IN BASEMENT

TAKE 2 1-2 HOURS ON JOB.

RUSH TO PHONES BIGGEST IN YEARS

ENGINEERS GATHER

OURY CLARIFIES SOVIET CHARGE

TRY RACE BET SUSPECTS

THOMPSON PLURALITY IS 65,000

HAS CABINET JOB THROUGH PRANK

RAISE JAIL MEAL PRICE

DEMAND BRIBERY QUIZ

ARREST MYERS

This *Hastings Tribune Extra* hit the streets within two hours after the robbery had occurred. *Courtesy of the* Hastings Tribune.

already been living there. He gathered up the clothes and turned them over to the police. Officers found that the suits were marked "L.C. Mills 9-12-29." Hendricks, a large man, soon claimed that the clothing belonged to him, even though the suits were of a much smaller size, which further aroused suspicions of police. The clothes were turned over to Hendricks.

The second report came from a *Tribune* newsboy. He told police that the people at the East Sixth Street house seemed suspicious. They had paid him for newspapers by passing the money through a window instead of the front door.

A final report dealing with the house came later that day from Arthur Lambirth, who worked for the Cowton Coal Company. After coaxing by ex-Hastings policeman Harry Wilson, Lambirth finally agreed to tell Chief Bramble about a delivery he had made to the East Sixth Street house. The occupants of the house had watched him closely the whole time. When he presented the bill to be signed, the front door opened only a crack and a gruff voice asked, "What do you want?" Robert Hendricks signed the form and told Lambirth to hurry up with the delivery. Additionally, a neighbor who lived near the house reported that a Chevrolet sedan drove into the garage at the house shortly after the discovery of the bank robbery.

About ten o'clock that night, Bramble decided that he wouldn't be able to sleep if he didn't have the house checked out before he went to bed. Apparently still believing that the occupants were probably just bootleggers, he remained at the station with Captain Frank Yetman and Sheriff Crosson. He sent two cars and several officers—Tommy Dryden, Melvin McGuire, James Wood, William O'Brien and Desk Sergeant Elbert Dailey—to the house. Kearney County sheriff Renus Kargo and his deputy Lars Johnson, who had come from Minden to assist in the search for the bandits, if needed, offered to go along, as did special officer Volcott Condit.

The officers noticed a Chevrolet and a Ford in the garage when they arrived at 810 East Sixth Street. Sergeant Dailey led Officer Wood and Sheriff Kargo to the front door. Officer Dryden and Condit positioned themselves at the back door (southwest corner), while McGuire, O'Brien and Deputy Johnson covered the other corners of the house.

The door was answered by a large man dressed in pajamas. Sergeant Dailey told the man they had come to check out the cars in the garage and asked to see their ownership papers. The man invited the officers inside, so they followed him through the small parlor into a dining room where a large dining table sat. He excused himself momentarily to get dressed. At that time, another man stepped into view, pointed a sawed-off shotgun at them and ordered the officers to sit on the floor and face the wall. The big man returned after getting dressed and took away the officer's side arms. Towels were draped over their heads so they could only listen to what was happening. The officers outside peeked through windows and saw the man in pajamas.

The hostage officers probably realized that what they had discovered was more than mere bootleggers. Their captors questioned them about how many officers were outside, but they refused to answer. Dailey later testified that Hendricks said, "I'll find out," and went down the steps that led to the rear door. Shots were heard, and Hendricks came back inside and laid on the bed and groaned. It became obvious that he had been wounded. Hendricks had first seen Officer McGuire outside the back door, and the two exchanged shots. McGuire missed, but Hendricks's load of buckshot smashed a window of the house next door. He then spotted Dryden and Condit, and again shots were traded. Dryden and Condit reported that the "big man" had fired first, at which point they returned fire with their revolvers, Dryden's a .45 and Condit's a .32-20.

Thus began a very dangerous time for the hostage officers. Enraged that the apparent boss of the gang was wounded, there was talk of killing the

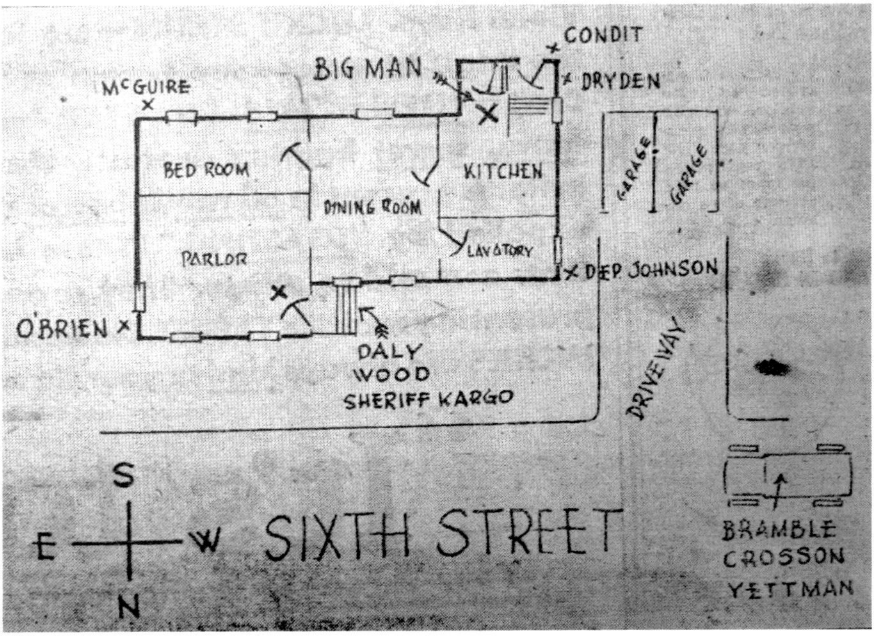

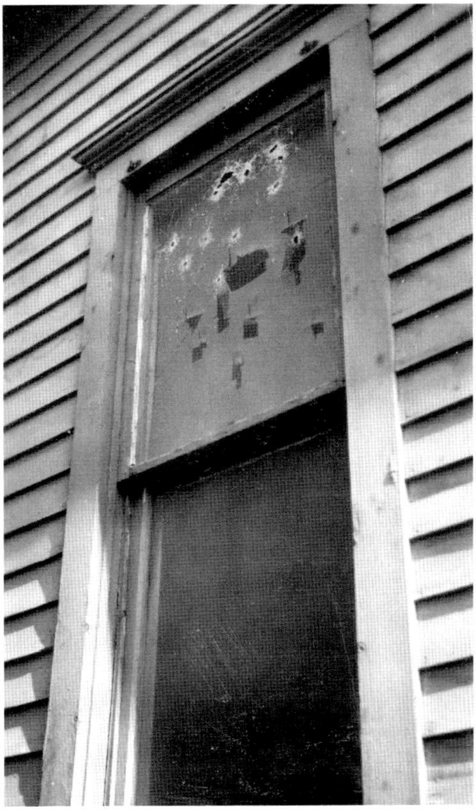

Above: Floor plan of the bandits' rented house at 810 East Sixth Street. Original positions of law enforcement officers are shown after their arrival at the house. *Courtesy of the* Hastings Tribune.

Right: Window of house next door (east) damaged by a shotgun blast during the shootout. *Courtesy of the* Hastings Tribune.

hostages. "Is Bob shot?" one asked. "Yeah, they got him," another replied, "He's been shot through the stomach." The two men, not knowing if their leader was dying, grew inflamed by the presence of the officers sitting on the floor. "What will we do with these fellows?" one of the gang asked. They became visibly excited and waved their guns around. "What are they in here for anyway? Shall we clean out the whole —— bunch?" The wounded man, identified as Robert Hendricks, finally spoke. "None of that, none of that, our job is to get out of this, and we won't do it that way. Don't lose your heads boys." The imminent danger to the hostages eased somewhat.

One of the gang grabbed Officer Wood and walked him down the steps to the back door. At gunpoint, Wood was forced to speak, "Come on in, boys, it's alright now." The officers asked who he was, and Wood kept repeating the same thing. The bandit holding Wood finally told him that if he didn't tell them who he was, he would kill him. He didn't comply, so the bandit opened fire with a shotgun. Two pellets struck Condit in the arm. Condit pleaded with Wood to make the man stop shooting. The man kept firing, and Wood said to the bandit, "My God, don't kill him in cold blood. Give him a chance to turn in his gun!" The bandit stopped shooting and ordered Condit to drop his gun and come inside the house, which he did. The gang then had four hostage officers.

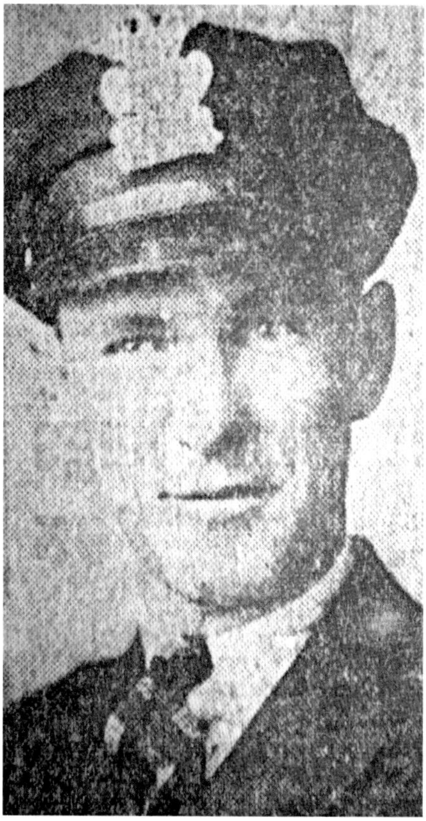

Hastings patrolman Thomas Dryden, a native of Brooklyn, New York, was one of the original group of officers to arrive at the bandits' house. *Courtesy of the* Hastings Tribune.

When the gunfire began, Officer O'Brien ran to a nearby house and telephoned headquarters. He told Chief Bramble, "Come quick, part of the officers are prisoners and the rest were being covered by a machine gun!"

Dryden said later, "When the 'big man' stepped out the back door and let loose with a Thompson submachine gun, we decided to change our position. I borrowed a .30-30 rifle from the Kearney County deputy and took a position beside the porch of a house across the street. Evidently they didn't see me beside the porch because they kept shooting directly at the house. The noise was terrific."

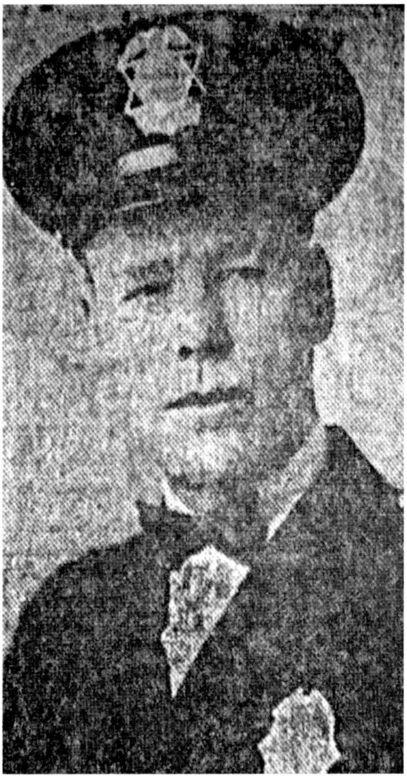

Patrolman William O'Brien went to a neighbor's house to phone for help after the shooting started. *Courtesy of the* Hastings Tribune.

As Chief Bramble, Sheriff Crosson, Captain Yetman and Night Sergeant Ray Thomas arrived, they saw machine-gun fire coming from the back door of the house. "We could hear the bullets pelting against the house back of us," Bramble said later. "I stepped from the car, I saw a fellow in a light shirt firing from the corner of the house, and I raised my gun to fire. But, just at that second, young Condit came out of the front door. He told us to put the guns in the cars, everything is alright, come in now." Bramble replied that he couldn't tell who was talking, and Condit identified himself. Bramble said, "Step out where I can see you then." The bandit holding a gun behind Condit ordered him to move out farther. At that point, the officers could plainly see the gun at his back. "Condit told us that the bandits were going to be white and that they had the rest of the boys in the house," Bramble said. The chief felt it was useless to open fire, as the machine gun would have wiped them all out. Bramble told the bandits that they would put their guns in the car. They did so and were ordered up to the front yard and told to lie down. One of the bandits went out to a police car and gathered up the officer's guns and car keys and returned to the house. Chief Bramble had arrived with his favorite sawed-off shotgun and two holstered revolvers, one on each hip. The bandits seized all the guns except Bramble's "$90 pearl handled, nickle plated revolver," which they dropped in their haste, the *Tribune* reported.

A bandit then kicked at Yetman's feet and ordered him to get into the bandits' Ford. Bramble's feet were kicked as well, and as he started to climb inside, his pocket full of shotgun shells thumped against the car and he was halted. "What have you got in your pocket?" the bandit asked. Bramble replied that they were only shotgun shells. The bandit then asked him if he was the sheriff, to which he replied in the negative. Bramble was then ordered back to the yard. Officer Wood was then chosen, his hands and feet bound, and he was placed in the backseat of the new black Chevrolet. Hendricks drove, with Mrs. Hendricks and their baby boy in the front seat. Bramble said later, "The car drove down to the corner without any lights, but I was able to catch the license number as they turned the corner and headed south."

After both bandit cars left, each with a hostage policeman, Bramble hurried back to headquarters to start calling area law enforcement agencies. In addition to giving descriptions of the bandits and their cars, he had to warn that they were heavily armed and that both cars carried a hostage officer.

CHAPTER 3

Mr. and Mrs. Robert Hendricks

I asked him if he was going to shoot me.
—Officer Wood, as reported in the Hastings Daily Tribune, *February 26, 1931*

News of the shocking gun battle on East Sixth Street spread through the community like wildfire. A huge crowd gathered in front of police headquarters. The taking of hostage policemen by the escaping bank bandits was troubling, especially to Chief Bramble. He felt some relief when he recalled that the bandits had treated their victims with a degree of kindness, more or less, at the bank. It was hoped that Officers Wood and Yetman would be released after the bandits were a safe distance from Hastings. Those citizens with automobiles who were gathered at the station were asked to head out in every direction to search for them.

The naysayers also made their presence felt. Some, apparently, were not happy with how the confrontation with the bandits was handled. No doubt Chief Bramble felt the brunt of their accusations. The *Hastings Democrat*, much to its credit, included an addendum to its article on the bank robbery and resulting gun fight on East Sixth Street:

> *Now that the battle with the bandits is history, there are a thousand or more people in these parts who can point out the mistakes made by the police. They can tell just what should have been done, and just how they would have performed the job. None of them, however, has a sub-machine gun jabbed in his ribs while he was pointing out the mistake. None of them*

had a pal or friend covered by ruthless bandits ready to kill at the slightest provocation. The house should have been riddled with bullets without warning. Of course the inmates might have been peaceful and law abiding, but why take the chance. The house could have been dynamited, of course. The two officers covered by bandit guns could have been sacrificed, of course; and Officer Condit could have been left to bleed to death while the other officers were searching for cars.

Thayer County sheriff Robert W. Geisler was one of many law enforcement officials who was notified by the state sheriff to watch for the escaping bandits. Thayer County, located on the southern Nebraska border, abutted Republic County, Kansas. U.S. Highway 81, which ran from the Canadian border to Texas, dissected the county. Hebron, the county seat, was about seventy miles southeast of Hastings. Soon after being notified, Sheriff Geisler and his deputy, Frank Baldwin, headed north to Belvidere and positioned themselves just south of the St. Joseph and Grand Island railroad depot to watch Highway 81, which at that time ran through town. At about 12:45 a.m., while talking with Belvidere marshal Charles Law, the three noticed headlights coming from the north and watched as a car pulled off Highway 81 into a closed filling station. They proceeded to the station and found a woman behind the wheel of a black Chevrolet sedan. When approached by the lawmen, the woman sped away. Geisler and Baldwin pursued her for two blocks to Second Street, where she turned west to head toward Hebron and points south. At the Burlington railroad tracks, the officers forced her car to the side and she was stopped. The driver identified herself as Mrs. Robert Hendricks. When confronted with the robbery accusation, she said, "Well, I didn't have anything to do with it but am in a bad jam, with bad luck." Her infant son was on the seat beside her; a man's overcoat and hat, plus a loaded .45 revolver, were found in the back seat. She was arrested, and Deputy Baldwin took them in her car to Hebron, where she was jailed.

Sheriff Geisler had awakened garage owner Fred Flessner to help him and Law search for a man Baldwin thought he saw get out of the car. The two officers noticed a flashlight being used in the hotel south of the Grand Island depot. They found the back door open and awakened the landlord, who told them no one had been up. Leaving the hotel, they heard Flessner yell, "Hands up! Stop!" The garage man found a wounded Robert Hendricks near the lumberyard south of the filling station. They searched Hendricks, who had only a flashlight on him. It was believed that Hendricks had been searching for medical attention for his gunshot wound. Geisler then arrested and transported

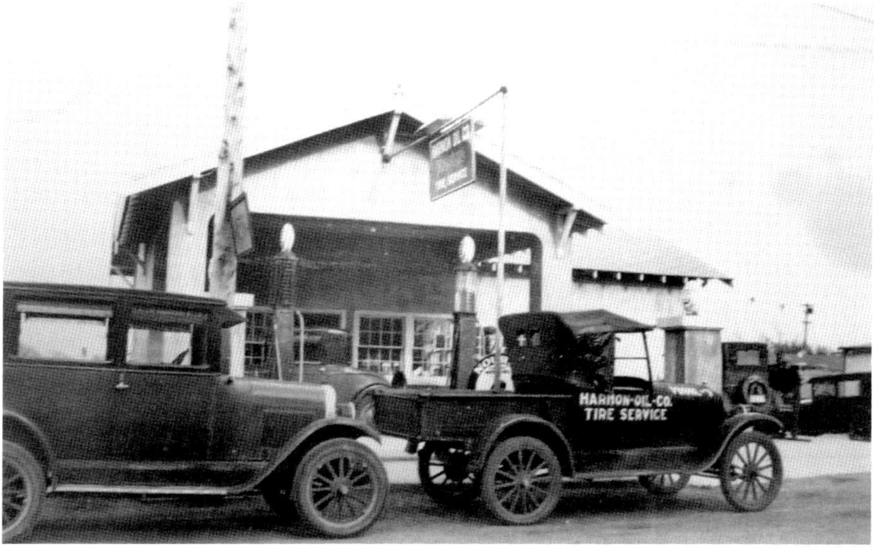

Filling station in Belvidere, Nebraska, where Jim Thomas and Velma Creighton stopped. *Courtesy of the Thayer County Museum.*

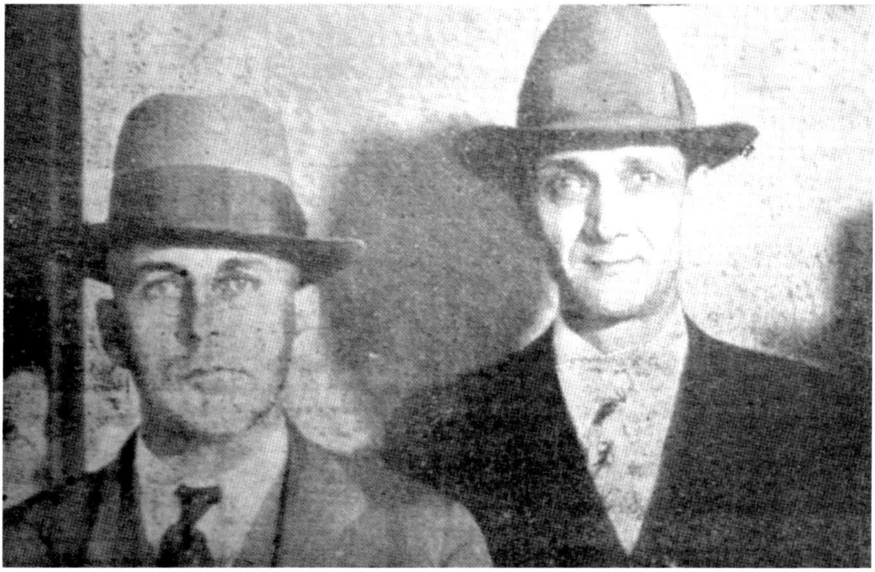

Thayer County sheriff Robert W. Geisler (right) with deputy F.E. Baldwin captured Jim Thomas and Velma Creighton at Belvidere, Nebraska. *Courtesy of the* Hastings Tribune.

him to the Blue Valley Hospital in Hebron. On the way, Hendricks attempted to slip the handcuffs off his wrists. At dawn, two reporters and a photographer from the *Omaha World Herald* flew to Hebron in one hour and twenty minutes. Hendricks resisted attempts to be photographed, and his hands had to be pulled from his face to get a shot.

Immediately upon notification by Sheriff Geisler that the Hendrickses were in custody, Chief Bramble, along with officers from Hastings, Grand Island and Worthy Wood, rushed to Hebron. The woman in custody said she was Robert Hendricks's wife. Bramble was able to gain information from her as to the approximate whereabouts of Officer James Wood. He called headquarters with a location on U.S. Highway 38 (now Highway 6) east of Sutton to search. A car sent out by Sheriff Crosson contained Art Bramble (Chief Bramble's brother), Officer O'Brien, citizens Grover Snell and Phil Lofing and Hall County sheriff Dan Sanders.

At about 4:25 a.m., the search party located Officer Wood four miles west of Grafton along Highway 38. His arms were bound to a telephone pole with barbed wire cut from a fence. The search party passed him by at first, but hearing a shout, they turned around and went back. Other than being exhausted and cold, Wood was unhurt. He explained his ordeal from the time he was taken from the house on East Sixth Street: "The bandit backed out of the garage and drove slowly down the boulevard to Second Street, not over 15 miles per hour. He turned east on the highway and did not drive rapidly. I asked the man if I could smoke and he said, 'No, I don't like it.' We never traveled over 40 miles an hour the entire way and when we reached the spot where I was found, the man stopped and turned out his lights. He ordered me to get out and told me to get a pair of pliers from under the front seat," Wood explained. "I asked him if he was going to shoot me and he replied that 'he should but guessed he would not.' He clipped barbed wire from the fence and then bound me to the post. He had two automatic revolvers, one in his hand and another lying across his lap. He then bound and gagged me. This was about 11 o'clock." Wood told how the bandit had taken off his Sam Browne (uniform gun belt) and used it to bind his hands and then had left. Numerous cars drove past while he was tied to the post, but Wood said he was unable to attract anyone's attention. He finally got his Sam Browne loose and threw it out in the road, but no one noticed it.

Chief Bramble and other officers returned Mrs. Hendricks and her baby to Hastings and placed them in the city jail. About 6:00 a.m., a phone call was received from Night Captain Frank Yetman to report that he was safe. He said that the two bandits who had taken him in the Model A Ford sedan

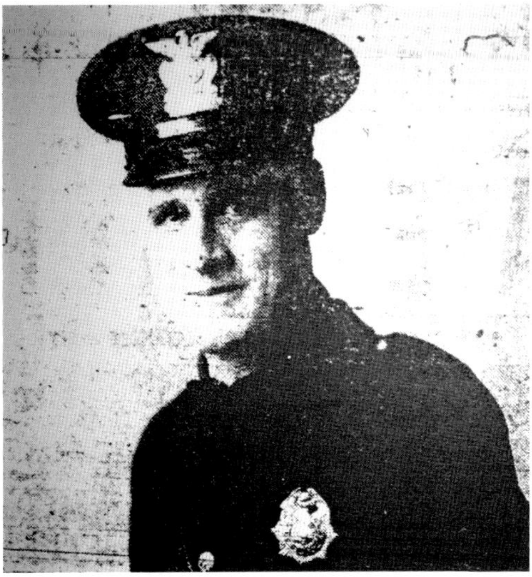

Patrolman James Wood was taken hostage by Thomas as they fled Hastings. He was later found unhurt, tied to a telephone pole near Grafton. *Courtesy of the* Hastings Tribune.

had tied him to a chair in a schoolhouse 10 miles south of Sylvan Grove, Kansas, about 125 miles south of Hastings.

Later, Yetman told reporters that the two bandits he was with had talked freely about the Hastings National Bank robbery during the ride southward. One astonishing item Yetman had learned was that they had planned to rob the First National Bank the very next morning while the police were busy looking for them. "They were pleasant to me all the time, and they kidded each other, back and forth, quite a lot. I sat in the front seat with the driver, and the other bandit sat behind me. I knew he had a gun on me all the time. The man who drove the car was called Bob. He was the husband of the woman who went with the other bandit—the man who took Wood—and he was worried about her. He kept talking about his wife and child all during the drive and said either they or someone would return after the woman and baby." When asked about the route taken, Yetman said, "We drove for about three hours, heading south most of the time. No one tried to stop us, although we went around the edges of several towns. The driver of the car was acquainted with every road in that part of Kansas, he even knew where the schoolhouse was. The car passed through only one town. They stopped at Hunter, Kansas, where the robbers broke into a filling station and stole some gas. Finally we came through Sylvan Grove, still going south. Bob said, 'Well, we'll have to get rid of you before daylight.'"

Ten miles south of Sylvan Grove, the bandits broke into a schoolhouse and took Yetman to the basement, where they tied him to a chair with rope. They told him someone would find him in a few hours and said good-bye. "I worked the rope loose in about 15 minutes, and started walking back to Sylvan Grove. Not a single car came along the road and it took me about two hours to walk it," Yetman said.

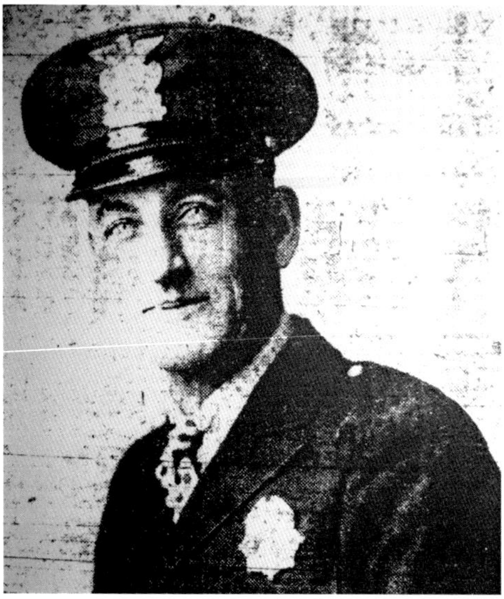

Captain Frank Yetman was taken hostage in the second bandit car driven by Jimmy Creighton. He was released in Kansas. *Courtesy of the* Hastings Tribune.

A.H. Jones, First National Bank president, offered a newspaper reporter his comments regarding the bandits' plan to rob his bank the following morning. In part he said, "While we know that no bank is entirely removed from the possibility of robbery, I believe that the information given to Officer Yetman was mostly braggadocio."

At 8:00 a.m. on that busy morning of Thursday, February 26, Chief Bramble telephoned Dr. W.I. McFarland at the Hebron hospital. Bramble was told that Robert Hendricks had "a small hole in the ninth rib on the right side," and the bullet could be felt under the skin of his back. The doctor felt that his condition was satisfactory to make the trip to Hastings in an ambulance, so Bramble dispatched the Livingston Brothers Funeral Home ambulance to go get him.

By mid-morning, Bramble had made arrangements with a local physician, Dr. E.C. Foote, who owned a Stinson-Detroiter airplane, to fly to Lincoln Center, Kansas, the nearest airfield, to pick up Captain Yetman. Officer Wheat accompanied Dr. Foote and another man on the trip. After picking up Yetman, they were to fly on to Wichita, Kansas, where they would compare information with detectives there. Yetman said later that he didn't know which was worse, being taken hostage by the bandits or the plane ride home.

A large crowd appeared in front of police headquarters by 12:45 p.m., anticipating the arrival of the ambulance carrying the wounded bandit. Shortly thereafter, the ambulance sped up to the station with siren blaring. A.J. Leonard was assisted with the stretcher by policemen and sheriff's officials as they carried it inside and up the stairs to the jail. Dr. McFarland from Hebron and a *Hastings Daily Tribune* reporter rode with Hendricks in the ambulance. Along with Hastings officers, Sheriff Geisler and four men escorted the ambulance.

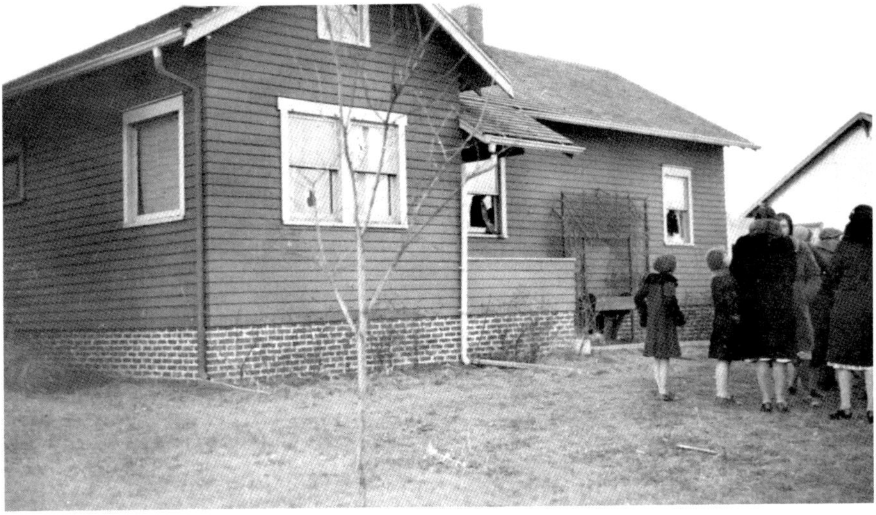

The day after the shootout, curiosity seekers milled around the yard of the bandits' house. Bullet holes and shot-out windows offered mute testimony to the previous night's events. *Courtesy of the Adams County Historical Society.*

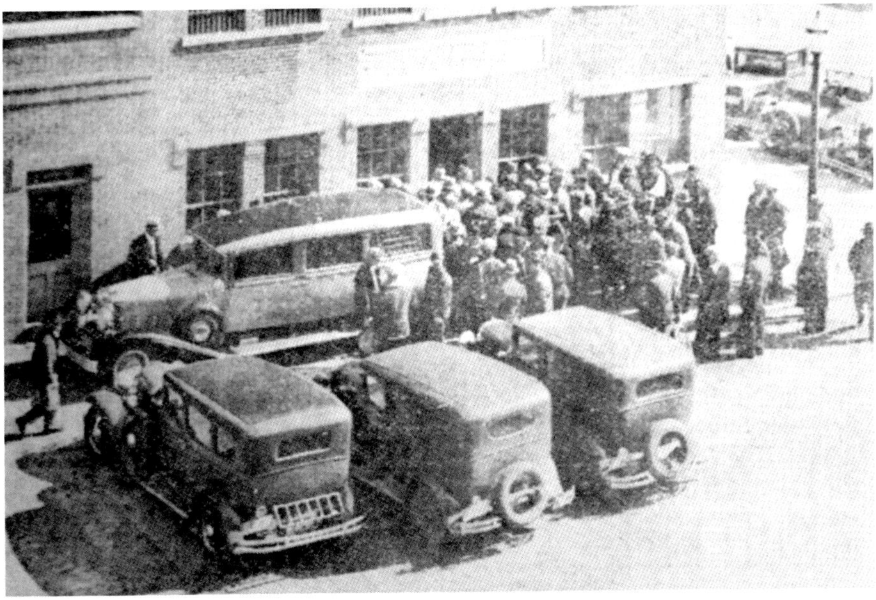

Onlookers at the Hastings police station try to steal a glance at wounded bank bandit Jim Thomas when he was returned from Hebron by the Livingston Brothers Funeral Home ambulance. *Courtesy of the* Hastings Tribune.

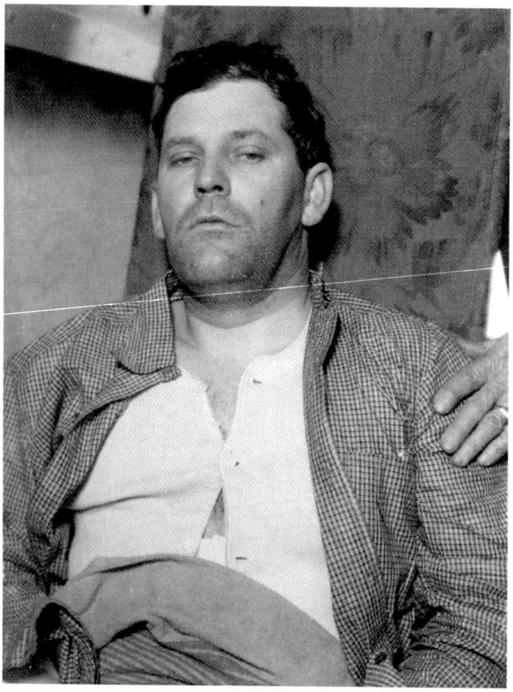

A wounded Jim Thomas is moved to an upright position for identification photos. *Courtesy of the* Hastings Tribune.

The crowd's hopes of stealing a glance at the bandit were dashed because a hospital blanket covered him from head to toe. Hastings National Bank vice-president, O.A. Riley, was among the onlookers. By taking Hendricks to the city jail instead of the hospital, Chief Bramble explained, "A saving could be effected in his care without endangering the man's life." The city physician had examined Hendricks before his stretcher was carried inside to make sure he didn't need immediate hospital care. The doctor indicated that the bullet had entered about three inches below the right breast, passed entirely through the body, punctured the liver and lodged a short way under the skin of the back. Hendricks volunteered, "I haven't spit up any blood." The doctor asked him if it hurt when he breathed. The bandit took a few long breaths and replied, "It hurts in my back."

Prisoners in the bullpen pressed their faces against the bars, as eager to see the bank robber as the crowd outside. Hendricks was placed in a women's cell next to Mrs. Hendricks. Although a steel partition separated the cells, an officer was posted to prevent any communication between the two. Bobby, the year-old infant of the Hendrickses, was then being cared for by Martha Wicker, service secretary of the Adams County Red Cross.

Robert Hendricks and his wife were questioned, but neither offered any information other than that he was thirty-five years of age. When asked where he had lived before coming to Hastings, Hendricks said simply, "I can't tell you." It was assumed that they originated from Oklahoma or Texas not only because of their accents but also because some of his clothing labels indicated they had come from those states. The bandit appeared to

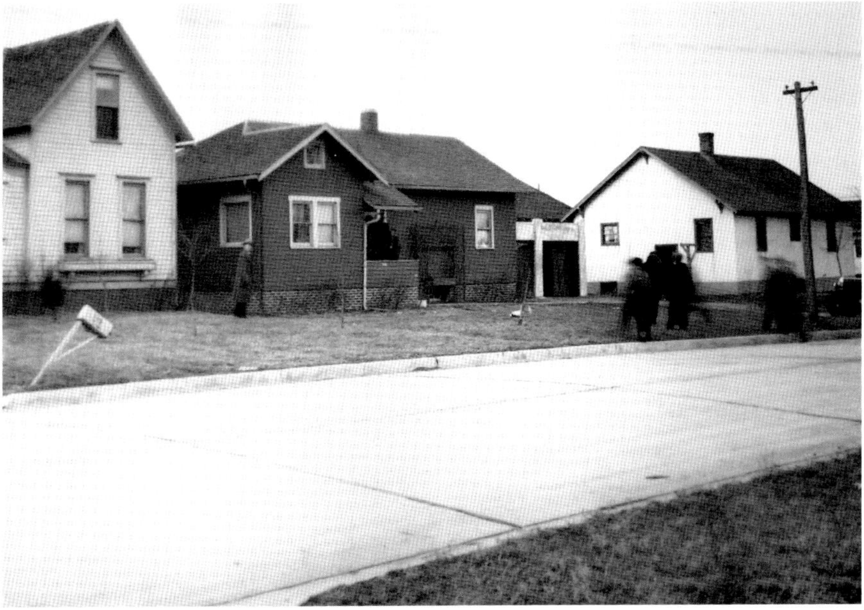

Officers reenact the events of the previous night at the bandits' house for reporters. *Courtesy of the* Hastings Tribune.

be concerned about his wife and stated, "Poor old girl, it's gonna be hard on her."

During the trip from Hebron to Hastings, the wounded bandit told the newspaper reporter, "I hope I didn't hurt anybody in the shooting last night. If the officer that the other fellows picked up don't get foolish[,] he will come out of it all right." He was correct, of course, as by that time Captain Yetman had notified police headquarters of his release. Hendricks told the reporter, "We got a kick out of reading about the bank robbery in Wednesday afternoon's paper." (They had subscribed to the *Tribune.*) Hendricks made a point of saying that he and his companions had planned to remain at the house for two or three days. He explained that they had intended to make preparations Wednesday night to be ready to leave at a moment's notice, just in case, but the police caught them before they had things ready.

When Hendricks was undressed at the Hebron hospital, five $20 bills were found in his sock. At that time it was also reported that $260 was found in the baby's clothing, and $850 was found in Mrs. Hendricks's coat. She also removed a $100 diamond ring from her finger and turned it over to Chief Bramble. It was believed that the ring had been taken from a safe deposit box during the bank robbery. (Ironically, a full-page ad for the bank in the 1930 Hastings city directory had proclaimed: "SAFETY BOXES—in our new modern fire and burglar proof vault.")

Robert Hendricks stated that Officer Wood's police hat and Captain Yetman's revolver had been left in the car. He said he had thrown the hat and gun into a creek just north of Geneva on Highway 81. A search party went out but was unable to find the hat or pistol. A leather rifle case that Hendricks had thrown out of the car near Strang was recovered, however. He revealed that he had momentarily eluded officers in Belvidere, when they captured his wife and child, by crawling into an old cellar. "I got so sick I thought I couldn't stand it any longer and decided to get out and find somebody who could help me." After leaving the cellar, Fred Flessner detained him until the sheriff and marshal arrived.

That afternoon, the black 1931 Chevrolet sedan used by Hendricks was brought to Hastings and impounded inside the Galloway Tire and Battery garage on West Second Street. Mechanics from the Hastings Chevrolet Sales Company recognized Hendricks's photo in the newspaper and reported that

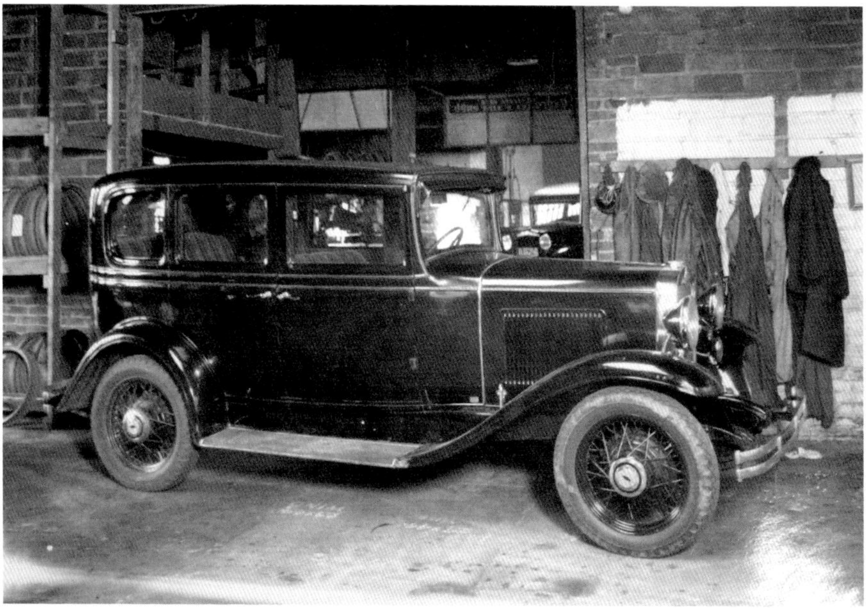

The 1931 Chevrolet sedan used by Jim Thomas and Velma Creighton, shown here after it was impounded inside the Galloway Tire and Battery Shop in Hastings. This is the car that "Mr. Cox" saw parked along the east side of the Hastings National Bank early on the morning of the robbery. *Courtesy of the* Hastings Tribune.

this man had brought the Chevrolet in for minor repairs and checks twice before the robbery. On at least one occasion, he gave the name "Wilson." Their service order indicated the same Kansas license plate number that the car wore when it was returned to Hastings. Bramble ordered a search of the car in hopes that the rest of the bank loot would be found. Officers checked the car's hubcaps, spare tire, pried under the roof and looked under the hood and dashboard, but they found nothing.

More successful was the search of the bandits' house at 810 East Sixth Street. Officers found $950, suitcases, grips and a large amount of new clothing. Some of the men's clothing was marked "E.D.D.X," some "L.C. Mills 9-12-29" and two garments were marked "Jimmie Giles." It appeared that the bandits had no intention of leaving immediately, as the clothing was not packed and infant garments were still on the backyard clothesline. Several rings of wire were found, similar to that used to bind the hands and feet of bank employees. A Remington .30-caliber automatic rifle was found, and a later check revealed that it had been shipped from Remington Arms to the Amarillo Hardware Company in Amarillo, Texas. Ammunition was found, but the rest of the bandits' guns and those of the policemen were gone.

Personal effects found included photographs that police hoped would help identify the suspects. A floor register was removed, and hidden inside were three sets of license plates, Hall and Lancaster County, Nebraska, and a pair from Texas. While officers searched inside, a somber crowd of onlookers milled around in the yard, looking at bullet holes and broken glass, which were mute testament to the gun battle the night before. A "For Rent" sign had appeared in a front window.

The *Tribune* photographers worked for hours to make copies of the photo that had been taken of the wounded Hendricks as soon as he arrived in Hastings. Prints were still wet when they were sent off by mail, train and airplane to regional newspapers and law enforcement agencies. Officers spent the day going through police photographs and Bertillon records supplied by the Nebraska Bankers Association. Fingerprints were lifted from the bank window entered by the bandits and compared to those records.

L.A. Woodley, of the famous William J. Burns International Detective Agency, arrived from their Kansas City office with photographs of known and wanted bank robbers. The Burns agency represented the American Bankers Protective Association. He showed them to bank employees and other witnesses, in case any looked familiar. Kearney County sheriff Renus Kargo thought he recognized a photo of Lonnie C. Mills, alias Clyde Nemerick, alias James Allen Woodruff, alias W.M. Mills. Kargo declared,

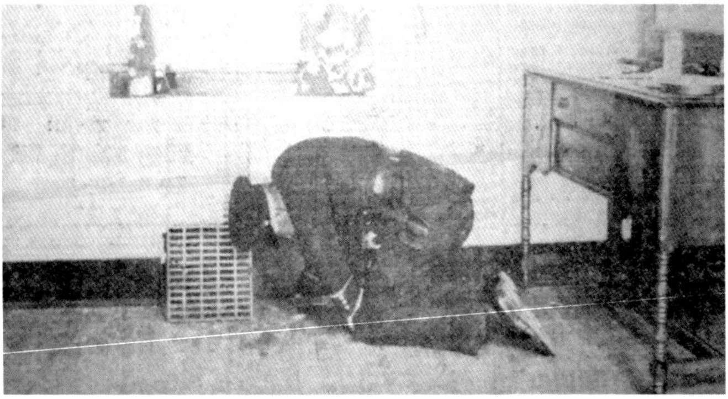

A Hastings policeman finds various sets of license plates hidden inside of a furnace grate while searching the bandit house for loot. *Courtesy of the* Hastings Tribune.

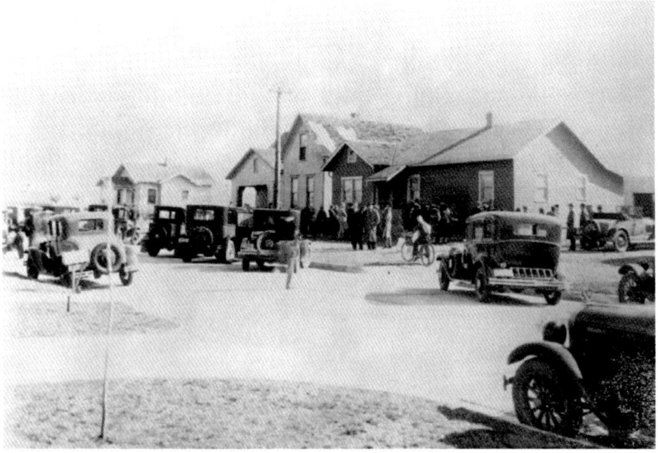

A crowd gathers outside while police search the bandits' house for evidence and stolen money. *Courtesy of the* Hastings Tribune.

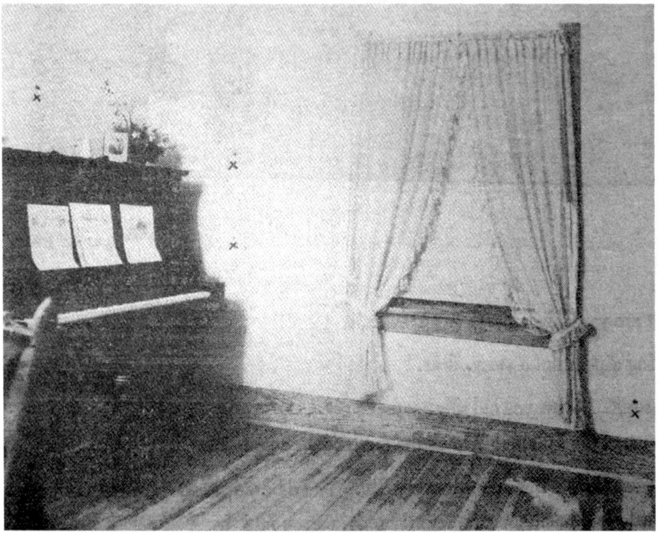

Front room of the home of Mr. and Mrs. R.E. Dearborn, directly across the street from the bandit house. The Xs indicate bullet holes. *Courtesy of the* Hastings Tribune.

"I'd swear that is the man who put a gun in my face." William Meininger, janitor of the bank, said, "That's the man, I'd bet my life." He claimed to be able to recognize the part of "Nemerick's" face that was not covered by a mask. Mrs. Blanche Pickard positively identified a photo of "Nemerick" and stated that he had called at her home next door to the bandit house to give her a key. It was never explained what the key was for.

Arthur Lambirth, who had delivered coal to the bandit house, was positive in his identification of one of the photos, that of James C. (Clyde) Thomas, alias Robert Hendricks. He explained that he had not only gotten a good look at Thomas but had also obtained his signature. Additionally, he well remembered the "severe cussing" he received because it took an hour to deliver the coal after they called in the order and said to hurry. Captain Yetman identified a photo of James Creighton, saying, "That's the man who drove the car [the Model A Ford that Yetman was taken away in]. He was pretty tough."

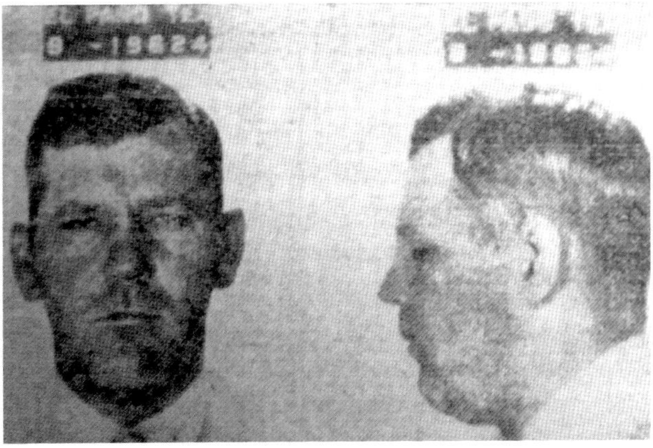

James Clyde Thomas's mugshot from an arrest in El Paso, Texas, for violation of the Volstead Act. *Courtesy of the* Hastings Tribune.

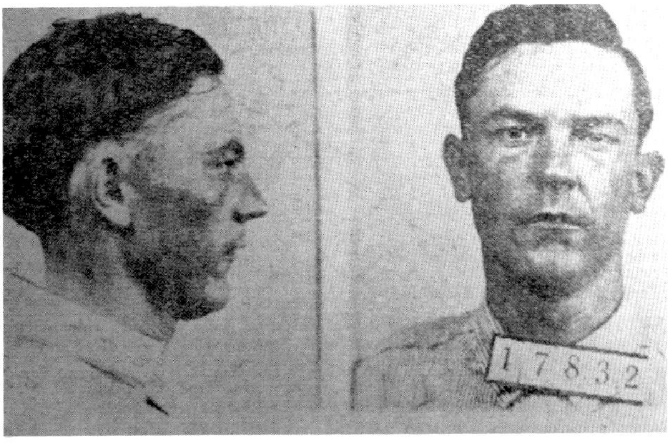

James Marvin Creighton. *Courtesy of the* Hastings Tribune.

A telegram from the police in Kansas City informed Hastings police that they held arrest warrants from Texas for James Thomas and James Creighton, alias Jimmie "Red" Giles, alias W.H. Geers, alias Jimmie Jones. They had apparently robbed a bank at Canyon, Texas, of $13,000 on January 10 before coming to Hastings. They were suspected of robbing banks at Kansas City and St. Joseph, Missouri, as well.

With information received about "Mrs. Hendricks" from Captain Yetman upon his arrival back in Hastings, and with the identity of Thomas and Creighton established, she was confronted. No longer trying to bluff, she readily admitted that her name was Velma M. Creighton, wife of James Creighton.

She did, however, maintain her innocence, as well as that of her husband and the men with him. She said she thought her husband was a common laborer. William C. Condit (past state sheriff and father of Volcott) asked, "What kind of labor did you think your husband was doing?" She replied that he had been out of work for awhile. She maintained that she didn't know there was a machine gun in the house or any luggage or clothing other than her own. Officers must have wondered: why then, if she was innocent of all that was going on, did she come to Hastings with another man, use an alias and represent herself as the wife of that man?

The *Tribune* declared that there had been other major robberies in this region where the escape of the bandits was complete and the loss of the loot clean. "Not so in the Hastings episode."

CHAPTER 4

Who Were Those Masked Men?

I didn't want to kill any of you boys.
—James Clyde Thomas, as reported in the Lincoln Star, *March 3, 1931*

City Physician J.P. Feese announced on the morning of Friday, February 27, that unless wounded bank robber Jim Thomas's condition changed quickly for the better, he would not live but two or three more days. Just before noon, an ambulance was summoned to the police station. A huge crowd gathered in front of the station house when Thomas was carried out on a stretcher and loaded into the ambulance.

A police car led the way to Mary Lanning Memorial Hospital. Doctors there immediately removed the bullet that rested under the skin of his back and said that if Thomas lived until 5:00 p.m., his chances for survival would be fair. The .32-20 caliber bullet recovered confirmed which officer's gun it came from. During the exchange of shots between Thomas, special bank Officer Condit (both being wounded) and Officer Dryden at the rear door of the house, Dryden had used a .45 and Condit a .32-20. Officers Tommy Dryden and Melvin McGuire were then posted at Thomas's hospital room door to guard the suspect.

Adams County attorney Herman G. Schroeder filed five charges against James Thomas: bank robbery (ten to twenty-five years); breaking and entering (six months to ten years); grand larceny (one to seven years); shooting with intent to kill (one to twenty years); and kidnapping (life imprisonment). Velma Creighton, who was pregnant (she saw local doctor L.A. Swanson

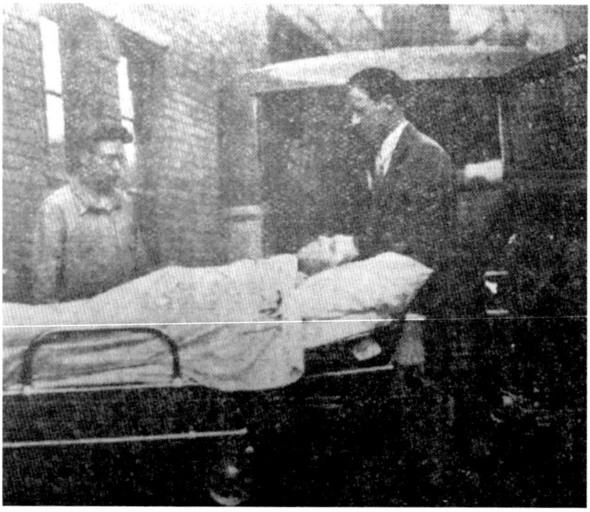

Left: Jim Thomas being carried out of the Hastings police station to an awaiting ambulance. He was transferred to Mary Lanning Memorial Hospital as his condition worsened. *Courtesy of the* Hastings Tribune.

Below: Officers Tommy Dryden and Melvin McGuire guarding Jim Thomas's hospital room. *Courtesy of the* Hastings Tribune.

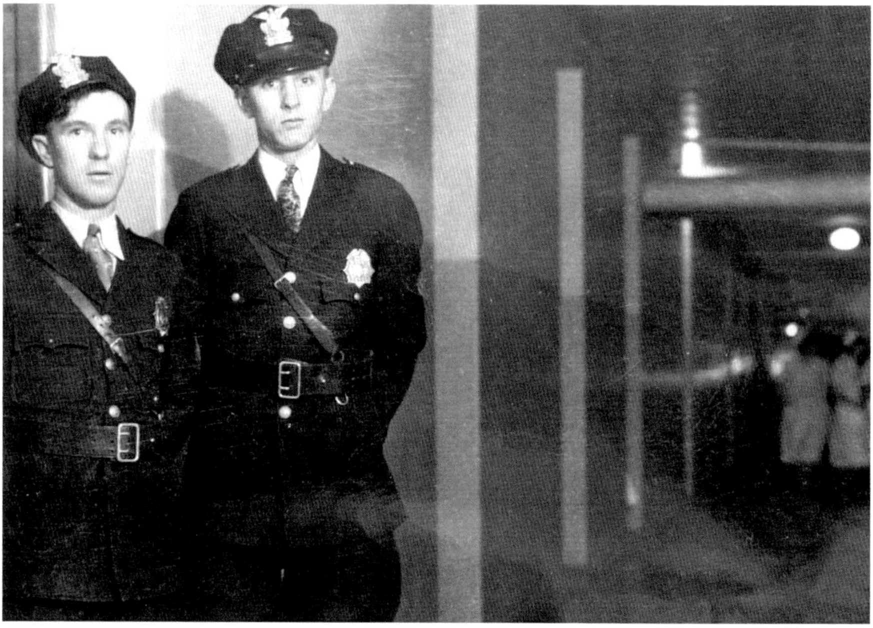

for an exam ten days prior to the robbery), was charged with three counts: receiving stolen property with intent to defraud, being an accessory to bank robbery and kidnapping.

The Burns detective agency records indicated that Thomas lived in Amarillo, Texas. This was later confirmed. Detectives speculated about a third bandit, who went by the name Cantrell, or as Wichita police suspected, a Virgil Johnson. Coincidentally, a man named Virgil Johnson had escaped from the Hastings State Hospital but wasn't connected to the robbery. The identity of the fourth man involved was not yet known.

The Burns files were full of interesting information about thirty-five-year-old James Clyde Thomas, who was believed to be "the brains of the gang." He and Creighton were known bank robbers. He was described as five feet eleven and a half inches tall and 180 pounds, with black hair and gray eyes. He had spent three years in a Texas prison for a 1917 auto theft in Waco (inmate #40463). When filling out his draft registration card on June 5, 1917, Thomas had listed his occupation as "Farmer-Convict." In 1919, at age twenty-four, he purchased the American Club at Ninth and Webster in Waco, Texas. At that time, Thomas was married to his first wife, Cora Hancock, and they lived at 1016 Washington Street.

Also shown was a 1929 arrest in Amarillo, Texas, for "swindling." It was believed that Thomas had been making $1,000 per week handling illicit liquor. He was reportedly worth $70,000 ($931,000 in today's dollars) at the time. On one occasion, he had been charged with blackmail and threatening to dynamite the homes of two prominent Waco citizens. Charges were dropped even though sticks of dynamite with fuse caps were found in his car and he had admitted that he intended to throw them under the homes if his demands were not met. Interestingly, in the early 1920s, Thomas had been captain of the West End Hook and Ladder Company No. 2, in Waco. The Burns agency reported that he was regarded as an extremely dangerous man.

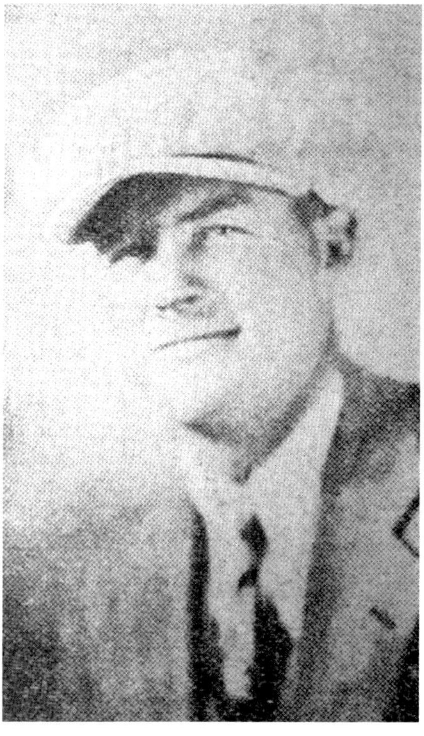

This photo of a slightly younger Jim Thomas was found at the bandits' house. *Courtesy of the* Hastings Tribune.

Thomas's mother, Minnie, was contacted by a Burns detective in Waco. She told him that she had seldom heard from her son and believed that he lived in Borger, Texas, where oil fields had recently opened.

James Marvin Creighton was described as about thirty years old and five feet eight inches tall, with brown hair, gray eyes and a dark complexion. He had served time at the Granite, Oklahoma state reformatory and at the McAlester "Big Mac," Oklahoma State Penitentiary on two occasions, serving five years for auto theft and two years for burglary. He was reportedly wanted by police in Tulsa, Enid and Seminole, Oklahoma, for charges that included safe cracking and robbery. It would be learned that Creighton was one of three suspects in a double murder (and possibly robbery) the previous year of two Connecticut businessmen at the Severs Hotel in Muskogee, Oklahoma, on the evening of April 26, 1930. A painter at the hotel identified a photo of Creighton as one of the strangers he saw hanging around the lobby on the afternoon of the murders. The hotel manager also thought Creighton looked like a man he saw in the lobby. One suspect was arrested and admitted to police that he, Creighton and another man had burglarized a business and stayed at a hotel in nearby Haskell, Oklahoma, on the night in question. This confession was meant to serve as an alibi for the murders. (The Severs Hotel murder case was never solved.)

More was being learned about the bandits' time in Hastings prior to the robbery. E.M. Foster, whose family lived across the alley behind the bandit house, said that his wife had invited the woman (Velma Creighton) to their home and his wife had been a guest at the bandit home. "My wife and I both thought she was very nice. We did wonder why it was that the men folks were so frequently away from home at night, leaving the lady and her baby at home." At one point "Mrs. Hendricks" told the Fosters that she was afraid at night, so they allowed their twelve-year-old daughter to spend the night. They were going to let her stay other nights, but their daughter said that she didn't like it there. The Fosters asked the lady what her husband did, but she evaded the question. Foster noticed that the men had been gone every night that past week until 4:00 or 5:00 a.m. and thought they might be gamblers. During the shootout with police, Foster had stepped out of his house to see what was going on and was nicked on the head by a piece of buckshot.

Velma Creighton's fears of being alone at night must have continued because she hired seventeen-year-old Lita Pearson to stay nights with her, paying her $2.50 per week. Lita said she was told that the lady's husband and half-brother were looking for a location for a drugstore and that was why they were gone so much. "Sometimes we went to a show, but most of the time we stayed at home. When we did that, she would crochet and I would read." When asked if she thought the "Hendrickses" were well-to-do, she replied that she did not, as "Mrs. Hendricks's clothes were of a very modest type." She said that the reason Mrs. Hendricks was afraid to stay alone at night was that the two houses on either side of their house were empty, and "the woman had a horror of vacant houses." Lita was told on the Sunday before the robbery that she wouldn't be needed to sit with Mrs. Hendricks anymore.

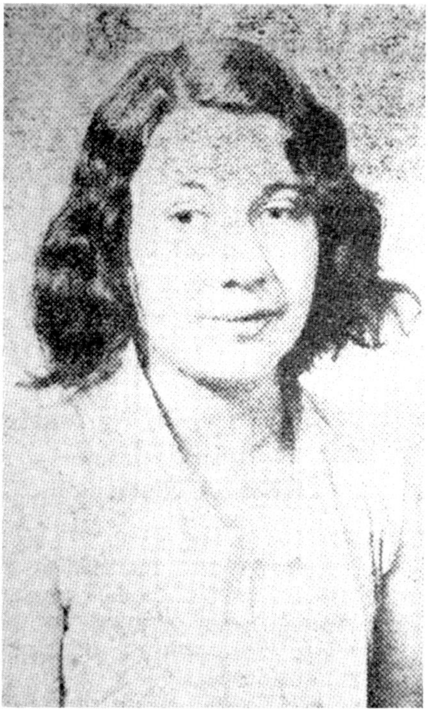

Lita Pearson, the seventeen-year-old girl who Velma Creighton hired to stay with her on nights when the men were gone. *Courtesy of the* Hastings Tribune.

Queen City Laundry employees added to the story when they reported that members of the Thomas gang had brought laundry in on February 3, 9 and 14, giving the name "Downs." On one occasion, a fifty-dollar bill had been offered for payment. This was so unusual that the young clerk had to ask her boss for permission to cash it.

The First National Bank of LeRoy, in southeast Kansas, had been robbed of $5,000 by three men. Police entertained the possibility that the robbery had been committed by the Hastings bandits due to some similarities of execution.

Doctor E.C. Foote's airplane was once again enlisted to aid in the investigation and carried Chief Bramble and Captain Yetman to Wichita to examine leads. They would then fly on to Amarillo to interview Jim Thomas's wife, Adelle. The *Hastings Tribune* chartered John Kline's Great Lakes biplane to carry a reporter along for the hunt.

On Friday, Mayor Joe Davis's eleven-year-old son, Leon, tried to persuade his father to let him search the bandits' car for the stolen loot. He had been keenly following the big bank robbery case that his father, as mayor, was involved in. It's likely that Leon's father told his eager son that the police had already thoroughly searched the car but hadn't found any hidden cache of money. Not to be dissuaded, Leon, an avid reader of detective magazines, continued to harangue his father until he finally gave in at about 10:00 p.m. and agreed to take his son to Galloway's garage, where the car was impounded.

When they arrived, Harve Galloway and Mayor Davis sat and talked in the office, while Leon climbed all over the new, black Chevrolet sedan. While in the back seat, Leon ran his hands between the seat and the seat back, feeling what he thought was a rope. In later years, Leon said, "I hollered, and they came running out of the office. I couldn't get the seat back out, so they got tools and removed some screws and pulled the cushion out. There was this tin box full of bundles of cash. My dad told me to walk down to the police station, which was only about two blocks away on Burlington, and tell only Chief Bramble. The other bandits hadn't been caught, and everyone was afraid that they were still around. As I started out, I saw bandits hiding behind everything. I ran all the way to the station!"

When Leon got to the station, he said that he asked for the chief, but the desk sergeant wouldn't admit him. "I told him my dad was the mayor, and he let me right in then! The chief and another officer took me out to a car and put me in the back seat. They handed me a shotgun to hold, so it looked like a carload of officers. We drove down First Street and went to the back of the garage. When the cops saw all the money, everybody was really scared. They thought some of the bad guys were still around. They took out the hidden box and the rope, which turned out to be a ladder, and took them to the police station where the newspaper took a picture with me and Dad and the cops. I wanted to keep the ladder as a souvenir, but they said no, because it was evidence."

The next day, the *Tribune* reported, "Acting on the suspicion that perhaps some of the money might still be hidden in the car, Mayor Joe Davis, Officer James Wood [one of the hostage officers] and Harve Galloway, in whose garage the car was stored, searched the machine and located the loot." The photo taken shortly after the find showed Adams County sheriff Crosson, Officer Wood, O.A. Riley (bank vice-president), Kearney County sheriff Kargo, Sergeant Dailey, William Condit, Mayor Joe Davis and eleven-year-old Leon Davis. The tin box, bundles of cash, boxes of gold coin and rope ladder were displayed for the photographer.

After the narrow tin box was unloaded, its contents were inventoried and the money counted. The cash, including five- and ten-dollar gold pieces, totaled $8,740. Also found in the box were drill bits, chisels and crowbars. This find brought the total money recovered to just over $10,000. It was believed the other bandits carried away the remainder of the $27,673.

James Thomas's condition continued to deteriorate Saturday. His doctors worried that pneumonia was developing because his lungs were filling up with fluid. By 2:00 p.m. they had little hope for his recovery. They did

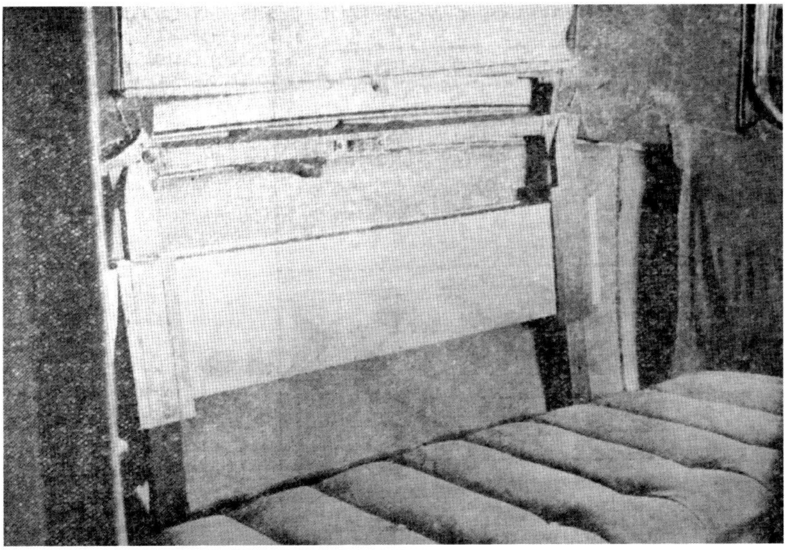

Above: Backseat of Thomas's 1931 Chevrolet with back cushion removed. The long, narrow container taken from the bank was installed to conceal $8,740 and burglar tools. *Courtesy of the* Hastings Tribune.

Below: Officials involved in the discovery of cash and burglar tools in the car pose for a news photographer with their find. *Back row, left to right:* Sheriff Raymond Crosson, Officer James Wood, bank vice-president O.A. Riley and Sheriff Renus Kargo. *Front row (holding rope ladder), left to right:* Mayor Joe Davis, his son Leon, Harve Galloway, Sergeant Elbert Daily and William Condit. *Courtesy of the* Hastings Tribune.

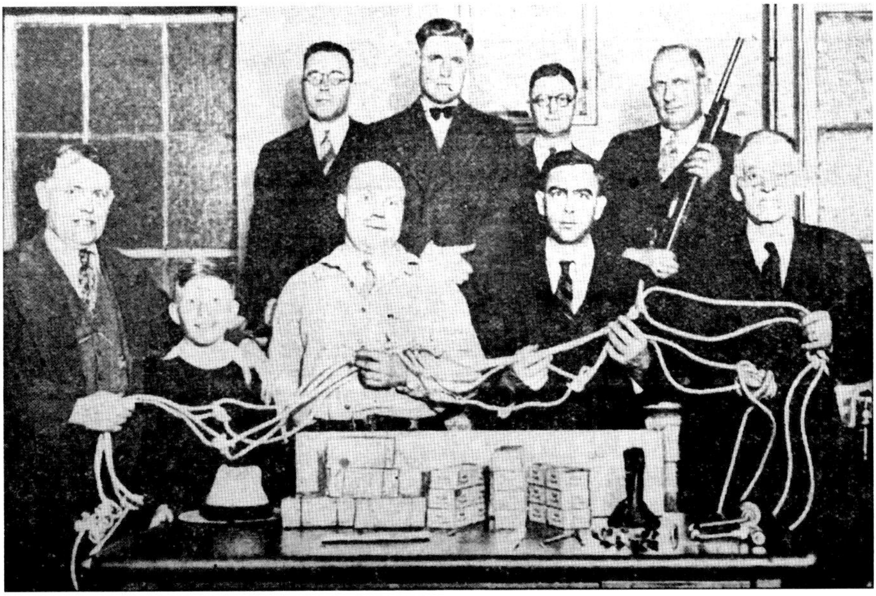

point out, though, that he had survived a very bad spell on Friday. It became questionable whether Amarillo district attorney Edward W. Thomerson, who was on his way to Hastings, would be able to carry out his mission. He planned to interview Thomas regarding the Canyon, Texas bank robbery in January.

Chief Bramble's party ran into an unexpected delay at Wichita. The Foote airplane had engine trouble, and by the time is was repaired, bad weather had appeared between them and Amarillo. They decided to head to Oklahoma City to check with police there. As the investigation continued, it was believed that the other three bandits had returned to their home stomping grounds of Oklahoma.

On Sunday, March 1, both planes returned to Hastings with all aboard, except for Chief Bramble, who stayed in Oklahoma to pursue leads. Desk Sergeant Elbert Dailey was appointed acting chief in Bramble's absence.

The following day, District Attorney Edward Thomerson and attorney Joe V. Moore arrived from Amarillo. Both requested private conferences with Thomas. Moore stated that he had been employed as counsel for the wounded man and Velma Creighton. Officers would not allow anyone to visit privately with Thomas, "no matter what their status in the case might be." This directive brought a stormy response from Moore. "Thomas," he declared, "has a constitutional right to talk privately with his counsel. If authorities here persist in refusing to permit me to see him, I shall go before the proper court and ask for a court order."

During an interview with a *Tribune* reporter, Moore explained that he had been counsel for Thomas on several previous occasions on bootlegging charges.

District Attorney Thomerson told the reporter, "Although Thomas is not known in Texas to be a gunman, he is known as a 'bad character' and as a man who possesses a wealth of nerve, plenty to resort to any means to get himself out of a corner." It was his desire to question Thomas about the other men involved with him in the Canyon, Texas bank robbery. Besides bank robbery, charges of kidnapping had also been filed. He said, "The kidnapping charge grew out of the fact that Thomas, with his companions, drove to the home of the Canyon bank cashier at 4:30 a.m. and forced him to accompany them to the bank and open the bank door for them. Then with the cashier in their custody, the bandits waited until the employees arrived. One by one, they held them up as they entered the door, just as I am told was done here." He added an observation that he made after visiting with Thomas (under guard by Hastings officers). "Thomas is not as sick a man as he would have those around him think he is." Thomerson had no plans to try to extradite Thomas to Texas to face charges there. He said, "If Nebraska gives him a long enough sentence, I would probably drop charges." He then returned to Texas.

In surprising secrecy, Thomas's not guilty plea was taken at his bedside, and Velma Creighton was escorted to county court, where her same plea was entered. It had been decided that the two suspects would be transported to the Nebraska State Penitentiary for safekeeping. Thomas's wife, Adelle, had traveled to Hastings and was given a short opportunity to have a few words and give her husband a kiss. She also gave him some flowers she'd purchased at a local florist. The Volland funeral home ambulance eased up to the back door of the hospital, Thomas was loaded and the ambulance then proceeded east to Lincoln. Cars loaded with heavily armed officers Dryden, O'Brien and Dailey, along with Sheriff Crosson, William Condit and four Hastings special officers followed the ambulance. Shortly afterward, Officer Wood, Policewoman Caroline Wahlquist and Velma Creighton headed east on Highway 38 (also known as the D.L.D., or Detroit-Lincoln-Denver road), to catch up to the caravan. Along the way, Velma thought about the kidnapping charge against her and smiled toward the "fine-looking officer driving the car," who had been her victim. She said, "The next time I kidnap a boy, it's going to be with his own free will!"

When Officer Wood caught up to the caravan, he pulled around and stopped in front of the ambulance to ask instructions. The officers following did not recognize the car, and two piled out with weapons at the ready. Officer Bill O'Brien, who rode inside the ambulance, said that Thomas didn't admit to anything but had said to him, "I didn't want to kill any of you boys. But this is my game, and that's yours."

Deputy Warden Dan Kavanaugh met the officers and new prisoners at about 4:30 p.m. at the east gate of the penitentiary, where the ambulance entered, and Thomas was lodged in the hospital unit. Creighton cried and held a handkerchief against her face, spoiling photographers' shots as she was taken through the north gate and into the female ward. Baby Bobby Creighton was still being

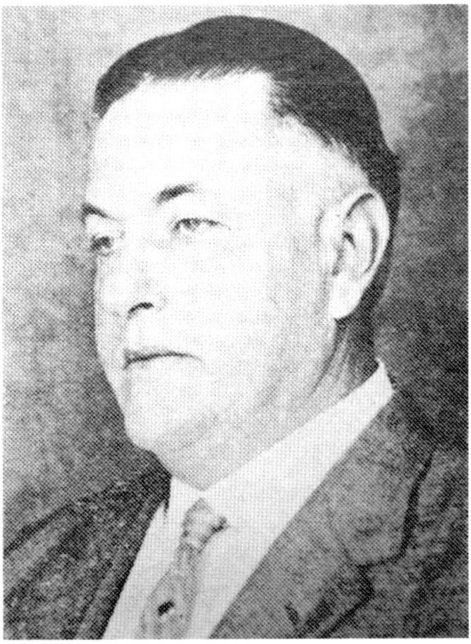

Deputy Warden Dan Kavanaugh of the Nebraska State Penitentiary. *Author's collection.*

cared for by the Hastings Red Cross. Cavanaugh explained to reporters that the reason private interviews had been denied to attorneys in Hastings was due to the lack of protective facilities. "At the penitentiary, the prisoner is placed in a wire screen cage and there is no danger," he said.

CHAPTER 5

The Hunt

Such, after all, is the glory of bank robbing.
—Adam Breede, editor of the Hastings Daily Tribune, *March 17, 1931*

Chief Bramble and Burns detective A.B. Cooper had been to Shawnee, Oklahoma, where Jimmy Creighton had lived previously. Creighton's record indicated that he had been held in the city jail on several occasions for petty offenses, but he had no county jail record. This no doubt indicates the beginning of Creighton's criminal career, probably as a teen. The officers were on the trail of Creighton and a man named Johnson who ran with him and who was considered a possible third suspect in the Hastings bank robbery. Also looking for Lonnie Mills, they proceeded to the home of Virgil Johnson (who was mentioned earlier by Wichita police), nine miles northwest of Longdale. There they arrested Bobbie Cubic on a liquor complaint and seized a still.

From Cubic, they learned that Virgil Johnson and his wife lived there and Jimmy Creighton had been staying with them. Their prisoner also told them Creighton and Johnson were joined by Jim Thomas the Sunday before the Hastings robbery. The following Thursday (the day after the Hastings bank robbery), Creighton and Johnson had returned to the house. Cubic had been ordered by Johnson to go get his wife and sister who were in Longdale and bring them back fast. Cubic said he did so, and after the Johnsons and Creighton had a private conversation, they offered Cubic the furniture in the house if he would pay the balance owed. He agreed, and the women left in the Johnsons' Studebaker Commander roadster while Creighton and Johnson left in a Ford (no doubt the second car used in Hastings). Before the two officers left Longdale, they checked with local merchants and found out that Mrs. Johnson had come to town and paid bills using gold.

The trail got warm again at a filling station three miles south of Tulsa. Bramble and Cooper learned from station operator "Whitey" White that Creighton and Johnson, whom he knew, bought gas and oil for the new Dodge "8" they were driving and paid him in gold. He said they went over to a nearby tourist park and called Tulsa. A short time later, two women arrived, and the four had a liquor party that lasted until 2:00 a.m., when they all left.

Late in the evening of Saturday, March 7, Chief Bramble notified his headquarters that he, the Cleveland County sheriff and detective Cooper had arrested Lonnie C. Mills at the farm of his sister and brother-in-law, seven miles south of Norman. According to the William Burns International Detective Agency, Lonnie C. ("Skeet") Mills was a known bandit from Garden City, Kansas, and used aliases like Clyde Nemerick, Allen Woodruff and W.M. Mills. Evidence of Mills's background appears to be substantiated by a court blotter in the *Chillicothe* (MO) *Constitution* on September 7, 1920: "The case of the state against John P. Ryan, John D. Allen, John C. Ryan, Clyde Nemerick and James Murray, charged with having burglar tools in their possession..."

Mills was then transported to Oklahoma City. An interesting item found on Mills was a note signed, "Mrs. Adelle Thomas." The note asked "Red" for money and said Jim was dying. Mills told Chief Bramble that upon getting the note from Mrs. Thomas, "Creighton wired $20 to Mills at Amarillo, Texas, and that he [Mills] delivered it to Mrs. Thomas." That was before Adelle Thomas headed for Hastings.

Mills denied any involvement with the Hastings bank robbery and said he'd never been to Nebraska. When asked to explain clothing with his name that was found in the Hastings house before Thomas and Velma Creighton moved in, he told Bramble that he and Jimmy Creighton had previously traded suits. Bramble explained later, "He says that he traded suits with Creighton, and that Creighton's suit fit without altering. That could not be, however, Mills evidently wants us to get it wrong about the size of Creighton." According to the chief, Creighton weighed 140 pounds and Mills only 118. Surprisingly, Mills admitted knowing Jim Thomas, Jimmy Creighton and Virgil Johnson, having been associated with them in the liquor (bootlegging) business. Mills knew about Jimmy Creighton's plans for the robbery of the

Bank of Earlsboro. Mills "snitched" and gave the officers the information (no doubt in hopes of getting a break), but their notification to local police arrived minutes late.

On Monday, March 9, the alarm sounded at the Bank of Earlsboro, Oklahoma, fourteen miles southwest of Shawnee. Two robbers had entered the bank as two employees were serving five customers. With guns drawn, they herded everyone into the vault. They were last seen heading east toward Seminole in a green automobile with $3,000 of the bank's money. Assistant cashier Charles Littleton identified a photograph of Jimmy Creighton as one of the two bandits. Detective Cooper and Chief Bramble joined in the hunt.

Two days later, the First National Bank of Harrah (about twenty-three miles northwest of Shawnee) was robbed by two men. This robbery didn't go as well. After forcing employees and customers to the floor and gathering between $2,000 and $3,000, one bandit made it to the green coupe (said to be similar to the Earlsboro getaway car) parked outside. When the second bandit exited the bank, gas station operator Walter Falwell shot and killed him.

The dead bandit was identified as twenty-year-old Denver Graham from Seminole. Found on Graham's body was $2,000 in cash, plus a bag with $500 in silver. Also found on him was an aluminum plate engraved, "This will bring you good luck." Within an hour, the Oklahoma Banker's Association paid Falwell a $250 reward for a dead bank robber. The Earlsboro banker tentatively identified Graham as Jimmy Creighton's partner, whom he saw in that robbery.

Chief Bramble returned to Hastings with Lonnie Mills on March 15. The very next day, the prisoner was moved from the city jail to the hospital. A sufferer of bronchial asthma, Mills had developed pneumonia.

Even though clothes were found in the bandit house bearing Mills's name and some claimed that they recognized Mills as being there, County Attorney Schroeder did not feel that he had strong enough evidence to try him on bank robbery charges. It is obvious Mills lied about the clothes being traded, as he was markedly smaller than Jimmy Creighton. He was at the house before and after Thomas and Velma Creighton rented it; he was later identified by a neighbor as the man from whom she received a key. He admitted to having been a member of "the gang," meaning with Thomas, Creighton and Johnson. He said, "Jim and I were partners until last fall." In fact, the big liquor racket that the two operated was still being talked about in the south.

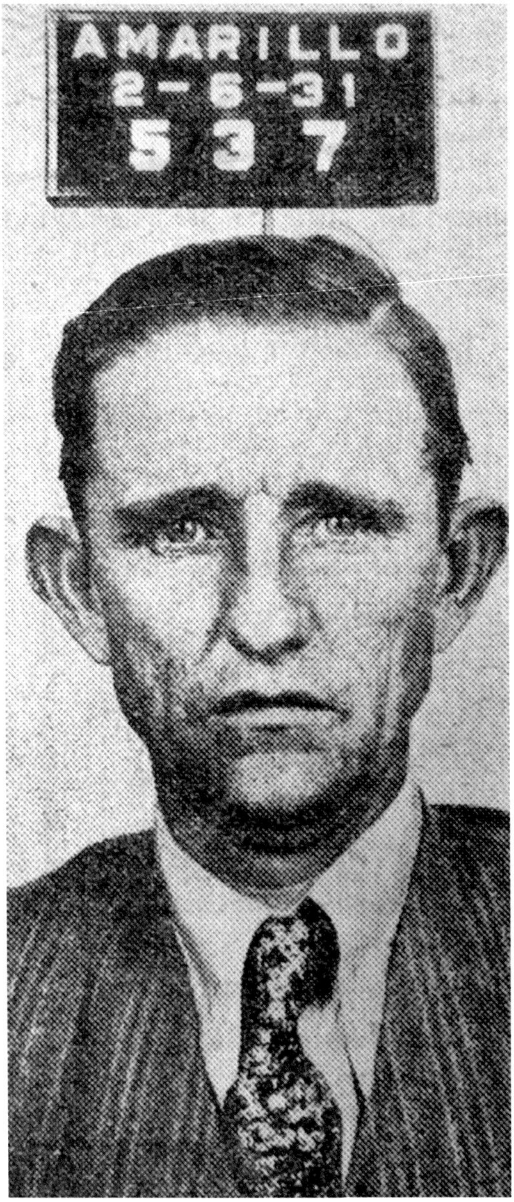

Lonnie C. Mills was arrested in Amarillo, Texas, in connection with the robbery of the bank at Canyon. Jim Thomas and Jimmy Creighton were living in Hastings at the time and were also named as suspects in the Canyon job. *Courtesy of the* Hastings Tribune.

The most reasonable explanation that none of the bank employees recognized his photo was because he was not at the bank. The *Lubbock (TX) Morning Avalanche* reported two days after the Hastings bank job that Jim Thomas and three others had been charged in the January 10 robbery of the Canyon, Texas bank. One of the gang, "Bill Mills" (Lonnie Mills), had been arrested for that job on February 6, two weeks *before* the Hastings robbery, and was still being held in Amarillo at the Potter County jail on February 27, two days *after* the Hastings crime.

On March 26, Lonnie Mills was released from the Hastings hospital and custody. After picking up money that his brother had wired to the local Western Union office, he caught the Burlington train No. 2 out of town.

Another look at the bank robbery was amusingly, albeit intuitively, written by Adam Breede, the editor of the *Hastings Daily Tribune*:

The bandits who honored Hastings with their visit gave proof that they are not the killing kind...unless necessary to do so in order

> *to get away. But as to ultimate killing, well, they were rather well supplied with the weapons of killing, which makes the strong suggestion that, polite even though they may be, they did not put killing entirely beyond the scope of their operations…And surely if one is caught it is better to be charged with robbery alone than to be charged with murder in addition. No, it is not to be concluded, just because a bandit does not kill when he has the opportunity, that it was a humane compassion that stayed his hand.*

Addressing the hunt, Breede wrote:

> *As we gather from the reports of officers, it is a territory of Oklahoma and Texas that is the habitat of many lawbreakers that sent adventuring bank bandits to disturb the peace and order of Hastings. From a territory where law violators are ready to help each other and to hide the pursued, came the marauders who scored rather less than 50 per cent* [sic] *success in the Hastings exploit…for their pain, they have lost a third or more of their loot, one of their number languishes with a bullet wound in the liver. Another, who would ordinarily be described as belonging to a nondescript class, has succumbed to pursuit…we see only those living by primitive skulking, and stealth in the dark, coming to prey upon the industry of a people that pursue the ordinary course of useful life. Those in captivity are in the position of a sorry lot, while those at large probably start from every shadow, as they flee from their fellows, as flee they will…such, after all, is the glory of bank robbing.*

CHAPTER 6

Jim Thomas, Trial and Escape

...the suggestion of cruelty around the mouth and in the eyes...
—Hastings Daily Tribune, *May 7, 1931*

A *Hastings Tribune* reporter called on Adelle Thomas for an interview at the Alexander Hotel. Adelle (Addie Lee Chapman) was Thomas's second wife; they were married in 1927. The woman was described as being "a strikingly pretty blonde woman whose eyes are blue, whose hair is golden and whose faith in her husband 'is stronger than my faith in God.'" She was twenty-four years old, five feet two inches tall, 120 pounds and dressed nicely but not extravagantly, wearing two rings with modest diamonds. She met the reporter's eyes when speaking to him, and her English and manners were noted as good. Talking about her husband, she said, "I love him with all my heart, and I'm very, very happy because he is still alive. In Amarillo, I couldn't sleep at night because I just knew he would die." She said that she and James have three children, two girls and a boy. About her brief visit with her husband at the hospital, she stated, "He was too sick to talk to me about the trouble he is in, but I just know that he isn't guilty." The reporter asked, "What if he went to prison for many years, would you wait for him?"

"Wait for him? Why, I'd wait for him always," was her quick reply. The reporter was persistent. He asked about her husband being gone for months, robbing a bank, shooting a detective and living with another woman he called his wife in a house for thirty days. "I'm not the least bit worried about that woman. I don't care if he did live in the same house with her. I know he was true to me. And, besides, wasn't there another man living at that house too? He was probably the woman's husband." Apparently amused by the conversation, the reporter noted that Mrs. Thomas was "not the least bit worried" about the other woman, but it wasn't entirely accurate to report that she was "not the least bit interested." "What does she look like? Is she pretty? Is she young?" Mrs. Thomas inquired.

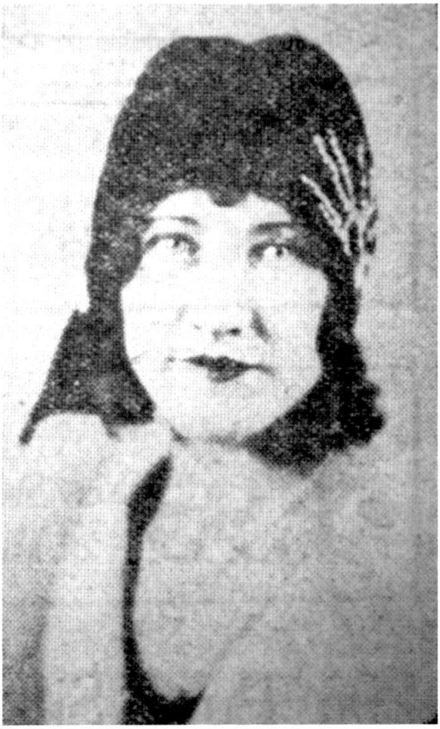

Jim Thomas's wife, Adelle. *Courtesy of the* Hastings Tribune.

Hastings attorney John Lawler was hired as co-counsel with Joe V. Moore of Amarillo. No doubt perturbed by not being allowed a private consultation with their clients and then learning that they had been secreted away to the penitentiary in Lincoln, the men appealed to County Attorney Schroeder. The county attorney supplied them each with letters to Warden William T. Fenton giving permission for Lawler, Moore and Mrs. Thomas to see the prisoners "at any time prison rules allow." They soon headed to Lincoln.

On March 10, Warden Fenton notified County Attorney Schroeder that it was the opinion of the prison hospital physician that, barring unseen circumstances, Thomas would recover. He would "celebrate" his thirty-sixth birthday inside prison walls. By mid-April, attorney John Lawler reported that his client had been battling influenza but was able to walk around his hospital room.

Inmate Velma Creighton had been allowed to post a $1,500 bond and go to her parents' home in Seminole, Oklahoma, as she was soon expecting.

The second week of April, former state sheriff William Condit notified Chief Bramble that a gang had been arrested in Texas and it was possible that Creighton and Johnson were in custody. Both Bramble and Officer McGuire remembered seeing marks on the face of suspect Johnson. (Apparently Johnson

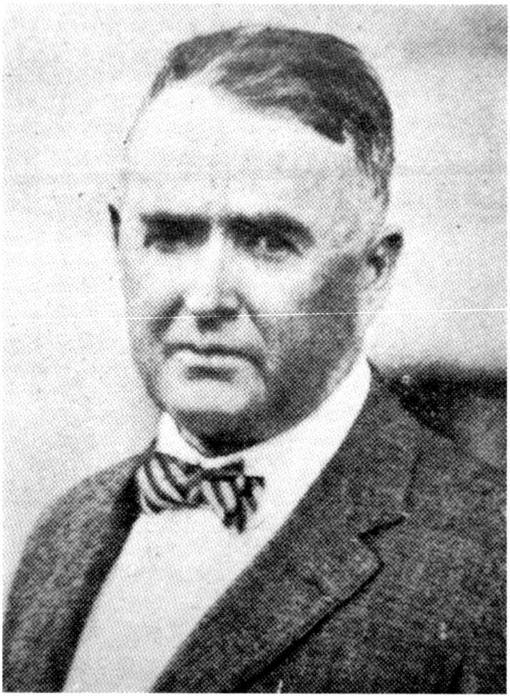

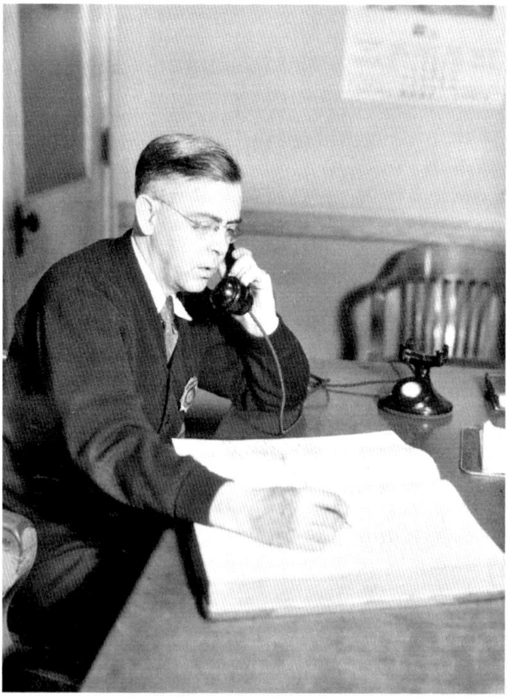

was considered a suspect by that time.) They were shown a photo of him and recognized him, but they had to wait five days before receiving photos of the gang arrested. One of the men was listed as "J.J. Miller," no doubt another alias. He was described as being five feet ten inches tall, with a dark complexion and dark brown hair. The officers thought Johnson had been shorter than that and had a lighter complexion. Bank employees also failed to identify his photo.

On Tuesday, April 14, newly elected mayor William Madgett was sworn in. This was his second time as mayor, having served sixteen years previously. One of his first acts was to appoint Sergeant Elbert A. Dailey acting police chief to replace Chief John Bramble. Dailey had been a member of the department since the mid-1920s. The game of politics

Top: Nebraska State Penitentiary warden William Fenton. *Courtesy of the* Hastings Tribune.

Left: Sergeant Elbert Daily was appointed police chief by new mayor William Madgett during the Hastings bank robbery investigation. *Courtesy of the* Hastings Tribune.

reared its ugly head. Actually, up until the 1950s, it was common that each new mayor would appoint his "own man" as police chief, as well as officers. This unfortunate method of awarding political "plums" interrupted operational continuity of the police force and knowledge of the job but was common across the country. Many police chiefs and sheriffs took office with no previous law enforcement experience whatsoever.

Madgett also replaced the city attorney and fire chief. He indicated his desire to replace three firemen as well but stated that he would not make any further appointments on that night. Faces of the councilmen indicated that not all were pleased with the announcement. No doubt the diligence shown by Bramble's investigation of the bank robbery was fresh on their minds. Some, however, may have been annoyed by his absence from the city.

Madgett asked the council, "Do you demand the appointment of a chief of police tonight, or will you wait?" It was indicated that they would wait. He asked the city clerk if Bramble had resigned and was told that he had not. Madgett replied, "I will appoint Sergeant E.A. Dailey as chief of police for fifteen days."

When Mayor Davis appointed John Bramble chief in 1929, the council refused to confirm the appointment for several months. Finally, in November of that year, a proposal was added to the ballot for approving municipal bonds for the airport. The added proposal read, "Shall the appointment of John F. Bramble as chief of police be confirmed?" He was finally confirmed by a vote of the people. Bramble had been a member of the police force in the mid-1920s and then served as an Adams County deputy sheriff before being appointed chief.

It was obvious that the *Hastings Daily Tribune* was not entirely on board with Madgett's change of police chief. Editorials ran that explained a wide range of required attributes a chief should have and discussed the election process of mayors, saying, "It is rather astonishing that we are able to find any to serve at all under the conditions that we provide, and as a rule, since we permit such things, we are much better served than we deserve…it might be a better plan if candidates announced their appointments before election and put the responsibility of approval or disapproval of their choice squarely to the voters."

Prison officials notified County Attorney Schroeder on April 23 that Thomas could make the trip to Hastings. Sheriff Crosson and other officers immediately brought the prisoner back and lodged him in the county jail. The very next day, Thomas was arraigned. He pled not guilty to all five counts and waived a preliminary hearing. Judge Halsey W. Bohlke set a $25,000 bond, said at the time to have been the largest surety ever required in an Adams County criminal case. Afterward, Thomas told a *Tribune* reporter that if the case were in Texas, he could raise three times that amount, as he had done so in liquor prosecutions there, but he was uncertain whether he could raise that amount in Nebraska. When asked how many times he had been charged with liquor violations, Thomas smiled and replied, "I'd have to check up for a long time back. I haven't kept track of them, but there's been plenty." He went on to say that he had good treatment at the state penitentiary. "This jail [county] is alright, but the quarters are a little cramped."

District Judge John W. James ruled that Thomas would be tried on Monday, May 4. Attorney John Lawler asked that two of the charges be dropped, as they grew out of a single act. Burglary and grand larceny were dropped, leaving bank robbery, shooting with intent to kill and kidnapping. Lawler also felt that the wording in the kidnapping charge—"J.L. Wood, then and there being a police officer in and for the city of Hastings"—would prejudice the jury against the defendant and asked that it be changed to read only "J.L. Wood." Judge James approved the change.

News was received that Jim Thomas was out on bond from federal liquor charges at El Paso. He had been arrested in August 1930 for importing liquor from Mexico and his $5,000 load confiscated. It was said that this was the largest seizure of the kind in that section. Federal authorities had learned of Thomas's bank robbery arrest and impending trial and had decided to drop the charges.

By 11:00 a.m. on May 4, a jury of twelve men was selected. John Lawler appeared as sole counsel for Thomas, as attorney Joe V. Moore of Amarillo was tied up with a trial there. Lawler's opening remarks included the admission that the defendant participated in the shooting at the East Sixth Street house and that he carried away James Wood. Lawler also told the jurors that if witnesses tell the entire story, "They will reveal that it was his [Thomas's] action in the house that saved the city of Hastings from having several funerals." He went on to deny that Thomas was one of the trio who robbed the bank. County Attorney Schroeder opened by telling the jury that the state would prove, through witness testimony and one witness's positive identification of Thomas, that he was indeed inside the bank. He would also prove that Thomas was the man who admitted officers to the East Sixth Street house and was the one who stripped them of their side arms and who left with Mrs. Creighton, the child and Wood in the Chevrolet that was seized at his arrest and brought back to Hastings, the car being the same one that some of the bank's money had been found hidden inside.

Trial was adjourned after opening remarks and began again at 1:30. Bank president Howard Pratt was the first witness called. He told basically the same story that the other bank witnesses would tell, of masked men greeting him inside the bank and ordering him downstairs. Besides the amount of money taken, he also testified that a diamond ring had been stolen. John Lawler objected to itemizing the loss, but Judge James overruled him. Pratt testified that his knowledge of the amounts taken was based on bank records. At 5:00 p.m., Judge James recessed the trial until the next morning.

On Tuesday morning, the trial continued. Jim Thomas sat with "stoic grace" and wore a neatly pressed suit with highly polished shoes. His expression was one of enjoyment, "although behind that mask there evidently lurked a picture of a probable prison term," the *Tribune* observed. For the second day, the district courtroom was full of spectators, making it standing-room only. Others peered through the open doors from the hallway.

The state was able to prove, "by witness testimony," that Thomas was in the bank. Janitor William Meininger pointed him out as one of the bandits who poked a gun into his side when he came to work. He explained that three men had met him at the door when he walked in, two of whom were masked, but Thomas wasn't. He told of visiting Thomas in the city jail the day after the robbery and asking him, "Do you know me?" Thomas replied that he did and had said, "I told you that we wouldn't hurt you, didn't I?" Sheriff Crosson and ex-police chief Bramble were present during this short conversation, Meininger said.

An unexpected score was made by the defense when Officer James Wood testified that Thomas was not the man who had shot and wounded Volcott Condit during the shootout on East Sixth Street. He said it was a man "whom I have not seen since that night." Volcott Condit said he believed Thomas *was* the one with whom he exchanged shots.

Chief Elbert Dailey testified that Thomas, in pajamas, was the man who opened the door of the bandit house and invited the three officers inside while he changed. Dailey said when they entered, another man stepped out, pointing a sawed-off shotgun at them. Thomas then took their guns. Dailey said he was one of the officers who brought Thomas back from the penitentiary and told him that he had a question for him, but he didn't have to answer if he didn't want to. "I asked him what he did after he was in the bank, whether he went straight to the East Sixth Street house with the others or whether he went out later alone." Thomas had replied, "I don't know if I should answer that question or not," but then he did: "I went to the house with the others after leaving the bank." Of course this testimony was full of objections by Lawler.

Bank cashier Ivan Riley identified the metal box that was found hidden inside Thomas's car. He stated that it was like the boxes that the bank kept its silver dollars in. He said they were marked "State Bank of Hastings" (remembering that the bank had changed hands shortly before the robbery). He pointed out the place where the name was stamped and indicated that it had been scratched away. He added that the bank's gold pouch also had the bank's name scratched off. (It wasn't clear whether the bank scratched off the names or the gang had done it.)

William Condit testified that he asked Thomas at the penitentiary if all the men entered the bank through the window. Thomas answered that not all of them did. This reply obviously indicated that one man stayed with the car, as "Mr. Cox" had initially reported.

At 11:20 a.m., after calling no witnesses, the defense rested. Lawler had relied instead on cross-examining the state's witnesses. Judge James excused the jury until 2:00 p.m., when final arguments would begin.

During final arguments, each side recapped what they believed were the high points of their case. County Attorney Schroeder said in part, "Now and then the state does get some breaks…it certainly got a break this time. Had not Thomas been careless with that mask, this case would have been much more difficult…" Lawler attacked the state's valuable witnesses first. "Why is it, that although high officials of the bank were called to testify, the state had to haul out the janitor to say that Thomas was the man?" He continued the attack with this contemptuous statement: "There are two men in this case who are mistaken, or worse than that. They are W.C. Condit and William Meininger." This brought about a sharp final rebuttal in which Schroeder reviewed the good character of both Condit and Meininger.

At 3:30 p.m., Judge James gave his instructions to the jury, and deliberations began. After an hour and a half, the jury had reached a verdict. When they were returned to the courtroom at 5:10, Thomas leaned over to the *Tribune* reporter sitting next to him and offered his opinion of the finding. Thomas's guess was apparently correct, as the jury found him guilty of robbing the Hastings National Bank on February 25. Lawler filed a motion for a new trial, which would be addressed in three days, on May 9, set by Judge James for sentencing.

A subsequent *Tribune* editorial made an astute observation:

> *Unlike many who appear in a similar situation, Thomas looked like a man of capability. An observer could scarcely escape the conclusion that if Thomas is a bank robber, he is a robber by choice. Well set up physically,*

> *and with an intelligent countenance, there is nothing repellent to the ordinary observer unless it be the suggestion of cruelty around the mouth and in the eyes. This suggestion, however*[,] *dispelled when he smiles.*

Jim Thomas wasted no time during those three nights. An unknown person had secreted a small saw and thirty-five dollars in cash to him in his basement jail cell. He sawed through the short bars on the cell door window and bent them upward, and at about 3:00 a.m. Saturday morning, he escaped. He went upstairs to the main door and saw too many cars outside. He decided to go to the back door and open and slam it shut to make officers think he left that way. Almost before the door clattered shut, Thomas heard officers running through the courthouse. He saw an open window at the treasurer's office and slipped inside. He quickly hid behind a stack of boxes behind the door just as officers came in. They looked through the office, gave the boxes a shove and left. Thomas decided to hide on the top shelf in a storage room, where he rearranged boxes so he could lay down behind them.

About 9:00 a.m., Sheriff Crosson came into the treasurer's office to search again. He noticed some boxes had been moved and asked Deputy Treasurer Julius Polenske about them. Polenske said he would look around again when he noticed boxes on the top shelf of a storage room were hanging over the edge. He stepped up on a shelf and looked over the misplaced boxes and saw a person's back. He casually got down and stated, "Nothing up there but papers." He stepped out, pointed to the shelf and whispered to Crosson, "There's a man up there." Deputy Floyd Arnold was summoned, and upon arrival, both men drew their pistols, and the sheriff ordered the person to come down. He waited and then added, "Come down or I'll shoot!" There still was no response. Either to elicit a response or due to the high level of excitement, Arnold fired a round into the floor. Thomas quickly replied, "Coming down, don't shoot." With him was his topcoat and a bundle that contained shirts, underwear, shaving equipment (all given to him by officials for his prison stay) and two photographs of his daughters, who were, according to reporters, with their mother in Amarillo. He was handcuffed and taken back to jail. Seeing a *Tribune* reporter on the way, he smiled and said, "Good morning."

Thomas would later say to the reporter, "Well, I didn't make it, did I? I guess that was my last chance. It's a cinch I won't be able to saw out of the big house!" The reporter asked if he had been nervous. Thomas replied, "Not a bit. The only time during the whole deal that I got nervous was when Arnold fired that shot. I knew he wasn't trying to hit me, but I was afraid that Crosson might have thought that I fired the shot, and then might have

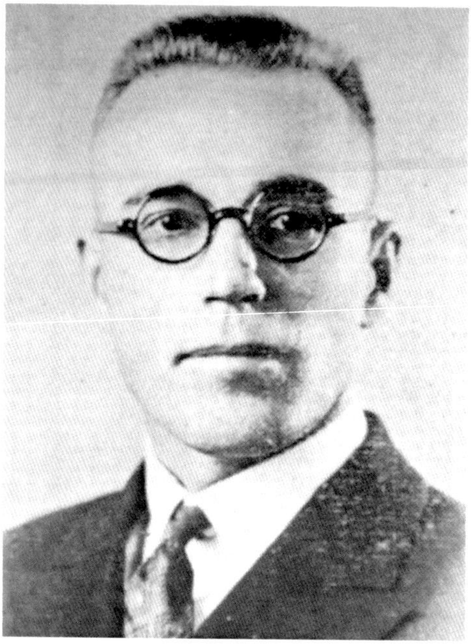

Adams County sheriff Raymond Crosson.
Author's collection.

plugged me." He said escaping was easy because he had been placed in the weakest part of the jail, the women's cell. Rain the first two nights had muffled the sounds of the saw. He said that he "forgot" where he got the saw and cash. Sheriff Crosson observed that Thomas had no visitors, but a wire screen over an outside window had been cut and was undoubtedly where the items came through. Addressing the saw and cash, Thomas said, "I had just as well say it was the third man in the bank job that helped me, because that's what the boys upstairs will think anyway. But it wasn't him, and I'm not saying who it was."

At this time, Sheriff Crosson revealed that just before Thomas's trial began, he received a letter from Texas. In it, he was told that members of Thomas's gang were going to "crash" the trial and take Thomas away. It made the assurance that the men coming were prepared to shoot it out if necessary. This was when he added night jail guard Charles Sherman, who, as it turned out, sounded the alarm when he heard footsteps on the main floor of the courthouse.

Within an hour's time, Thomas was standing before Judge James for sentencing. The *Tribune* reported that Thomas "did not exhibit the sartorial correctness that had marked his other appearances there." The defendant wore the same suit that he had on during the trial, but this time, instead of being neatly pressed, it was wrinkled and disheveled from hiding on the shelf in the treasurer's office for nearly six hours.

The judge promptly overruled Lawler's motion for a new trial and then took several minutes to reiterate the bank robbery charge, how the crime was carried out and the guilty verdict. He mentioned that although the shooting incident was not at the time in question, had there been loss of life, Thomas could be facing the electric chair instead of a prison sentence. The judge stated that he did not feel Thomas was a candidate for a lenient sentence,

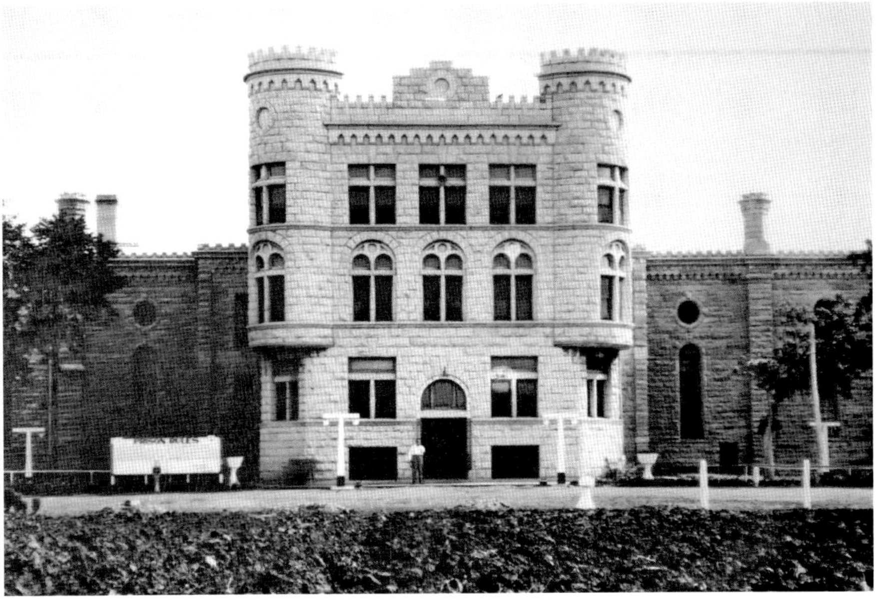

Above: Nebraska State Penitentiary, Lincoln. *Author's collection.*

Below: Newspaper photo collage of Jim Thomas's arrival at the Nebraska penitentiary. *Courtesy of the* Hastings Tribune.

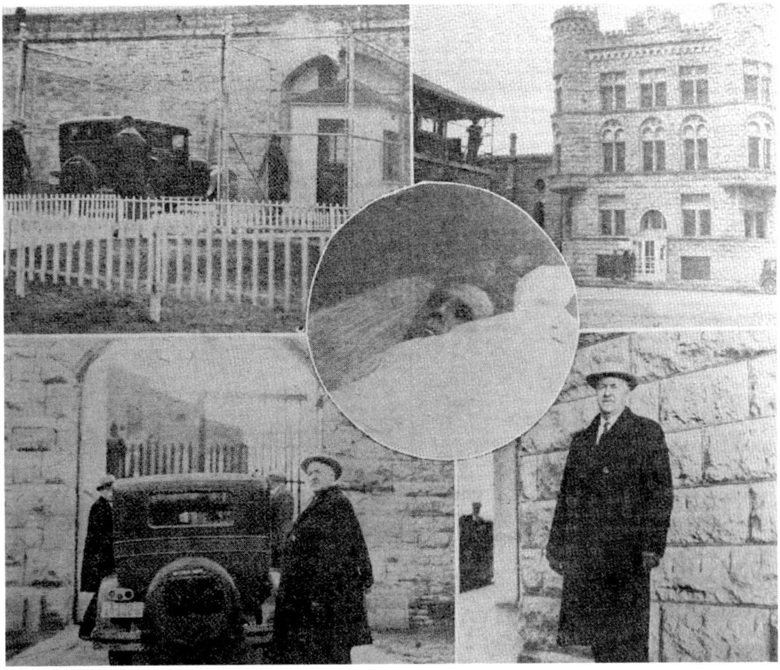

saying, "At your age, I do not feel that the question of reformation should be given very much consideration." He asked the defendant if he had anything to say before sentence was passed, to which Thomas replied, "Not a thing, Your Honor." The judge explained that what had transpired earlier that morning had nothing to do with his decision. "The sentence of this court will be, Mr. Thomas, that you be confined in the state penitentiary at Lincoln, Nebraska, at hard labor, Sundays and holidays excepted, for a period of twenty-five years [maximum penalty], and pay the costs of this prosecution. That no part of said confinement shall be in solitary confinement except for a violation of the prison rules. That will be the sentence. The sheriff will take charge of the defendant."

The crowd inside the courtroom was temporarily held while Thomas was taken out to Crosson's car, handcuffed to Deputy State Sheriff Fred Benton. A second car with more officers followed Crosson and Benton for the trip to Lincoln.

CHAPTER 7
Velma Creighton's Despicable Act

...the halo of motherhood...
—Hastings Daily Tribune, *October 21, 1931*

Two days after the bank robbery, Velma Creighton, alias Mrs. Robert Hendricks, sat in the city jail. It was her twenty-fourth birthday. Policewoman Caroline Wahlquist kept an eye on the bandit wife. Her one-year-old son, Bobby, was still under care of the Red Cross. In three months' time, Velma would give birth to her second child. She was described by the newspaper as, "a nice looking woman with black marcelled hair and a clear complexion."

"It's my first time in a thing like this, I'd never have been here if I'd known what was going on," Velma said. During questioning, she told William Condit that she wouldn't know a machine gun if she saw one, and neither would she know a shotgun or a pistol. She also denied any knowledge of the names of the other men who had lived at the East Sixth Street house. She was shown a pile of hats, coats and other clothing, most of which had labels cut from them, which were seized at the house. She denied knowing whether they were brought with them or if they showed up after they moved in. "They are not mine. I know nothing about them."

The arrival of Velma's mother and stepfather brought another chapter to the story. Mr. and Mrs. G.W. Humphrey visited with a newspaper reporter in John Lawler's office. The *Tribune* reporter noted that Mrs. Humphrey's "eyes[,] already inflamed from many hours of weeping, filled with tears again as she talked."

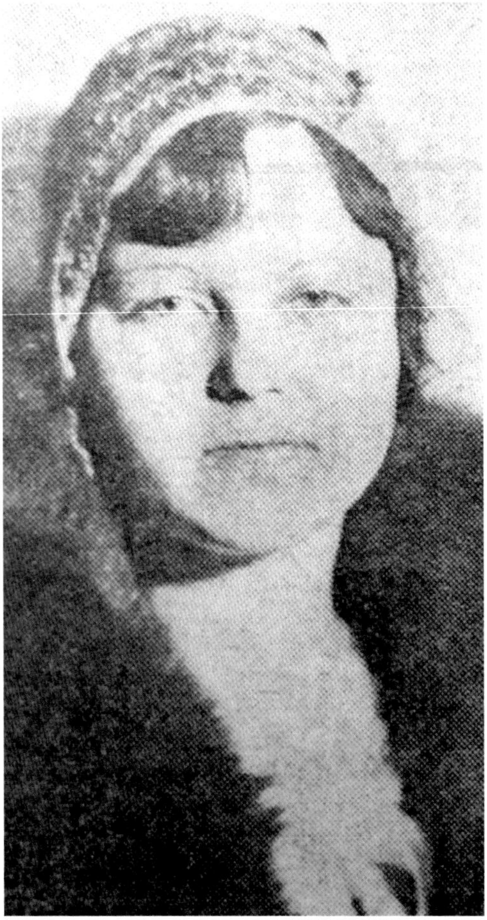

Jimmy Creighton's wife, Velma. *Courtesy of the* Hastings Tribune.

The distraught mother explained that Velma had not written to her in an effort to keep from hurting her. She only learned of her daughter's involvement in the crime from prominent coverage in Oklahoma newspapers. "Even yet I can't believe what I know is true. Velma was raised in a Christian home and has always been a model girl. The eldest of my three children, two girls and a boy, Velma prior to the time she married Creighton two years ago, had attended Sunday school and church throughout her life. Never had she been in any sort of trouble that would reflect upon her good name or mine," she sobbed.

The parents had come to Hastings to take baby Bobby home with them. Mrs. Humphrey explained, "When her father died some years ago, she immediately went to work to help me support our family. Each week she would turn her earnings over to me. Back in our hometown, all of our friends were shocked when they heard that Velma was involved in the bank robbery."

Mr. Humphrey told the reporter that he worked as a shoe repairman and that they were not well off financially, "but I am willing to spend our last cent to do what we can for Velma and I promise to amply provide for the baby." One of the photographs found inside the East Sixth Street house was of Mr. Humphrey holding the baby.

Mrs. Humphrey commented that she did not know Jimmy Creighton until her daughter had married him. She had not sanctioned the marriage as she said she didn't know about it until the ceremony was over. She added, "I

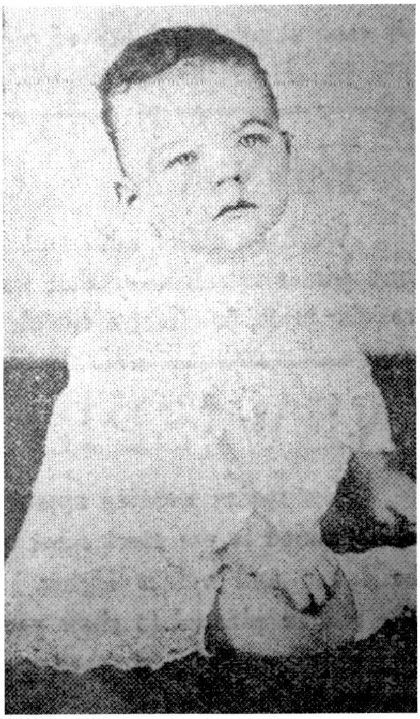

Right: Baby Bobby Creighton lived in the bandit house with his parents, Jimmy and Velma, and Jim Thomas. *Courtesy of the* Hastings Tribune.

Below: Velma Creighton's stepfather, G.W. Humphrey, holding baby Bobby. This was one of the photos found in the East Sixth Street house after the gun battle. *Courtesy of the* Hastings Tribune.

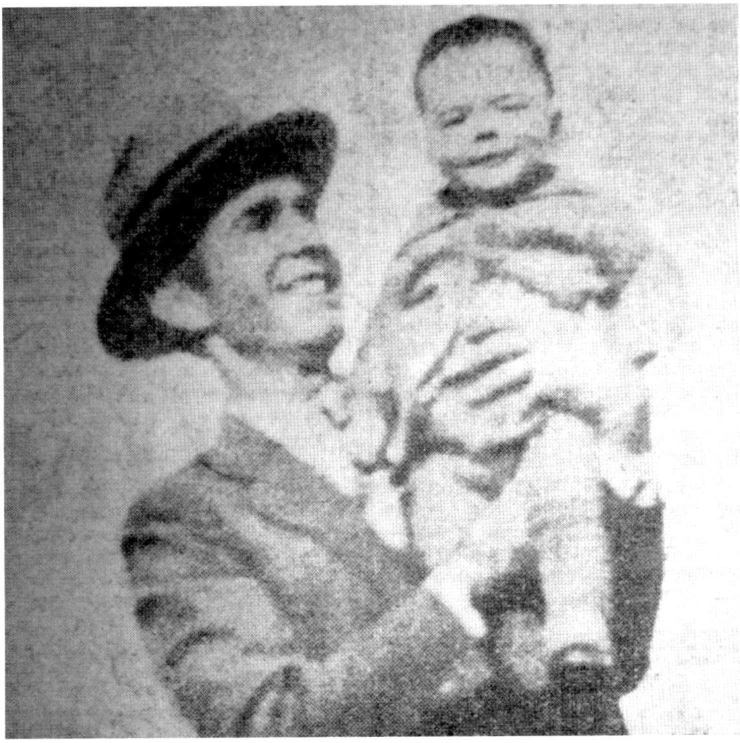

don't suppose it would have done any good for me to protest anyway, you know how young people are, if they get their head set on getting married there's no stopping them."

After the interview, attorneys Lawler and Joe Moore of Amarillo took the Humphreys to the penitentiary where Velma was being held for safekeeping. Once there, they asked Velma to sign a release so they could take the baby (who was then being cared for at the hospital) home with them. By the end of the week, with the release signed and approved by County Attorney Schroeder, the Humphreys left Hastings by train. Schroeder was told by the Seminole police that the Humphreys were the proper persons to have custody of the child.

Also during that busy week in March, authorities had established that Adelle Thomas was the legal owner of the 1931 Chevrolet sedan that was used in the bank robbery. It had been licensed in her name on January 10 in Texas, the same day as the Canyon bank robbery. Before Mrs. Thomas and attorney Moore left for Amarillo, she was required to get new Nebraska license plates, as her Texas plates were being held as evidence.

The Hastings National Bank, to further reassure its customers, ran a large ad in the newspaper that displayed a copy of the check for $27,773 that it received from the National Union Indemnity Company of Pittsburgh. In large type it read, "Our bank is not absolutely bandit proof, however the insurance we carry guarantees against loss by robbery."

On Monday, March 21, Velma Creighton appeared in county court before Judge W. Halsey Bohlke for arraignment. County Attorney Herman Schroeder read the charges: Count 1. Receiving stolen property ($810.00 of the bank's money) with intent to defraud; Count 2. Concealing a felony; Count 3. Kidnapping. The money was introduced as evidence, and she pled not guilty to all charges. Velma's defense team had grown to four with the addition of Fred Apt and A.R. Enfield of Iola, Kansas. They had been engaged by the Humphreys.

Nine witnesses were called and testified to the events of February 25. Officer Wood explained that when he and the other officers were captured inside the bandit house, Velma stepped out of a room, hat and coat on, and a baby in her arms, ready to leave. When Schroeder asked if she was forced to go, Wood answered, "She went without force." Testimony was presented by officers that several $50 and $20 bills were found sewn into the lining of Velma's coat, and John Bramble told of finding $260 in the baby's clothes at Hebron. At that time, she said to him, "That hasn't anything to do with that job up there." She had told news reporters that she knew nothing about the cash. Attorney Apt pointed out Velma's physical condition when he asked Bramble if he had jerked her ring from her finger. The ex-chief answered, "I did not, she held her finger out and I removed it."

With testimony finished, Judge Bohlke ruled that sufficient evidence had been presented to warrant the defendant be bound over to District Court for trial and set a $10,000 bond. Apparently Creighton's legal name was Thelma, but she went by and was commonly known as Velma. All Adams County court records reflect her name as Thelma.

On April 4, Judge James granted a request by the defense for a lower bond and set it at $1,500, which was posted. Velma was released to go home to Seminole, where in late May, she gave birth to another baby boy. The new arrival was named "Jimmy" after his father. The judge moved Velma's case to the fall term and set trial for October 19.

In an effort to substantiate a lack of wrongdoing on Velma's part, the defense filed a motion to take a deposition from James Thomas at the penitentiary. This was done on October 14 with County Attorney Herman Schroeder appearing for the state and John Lawler for the defense.

Thomas said he had known Velma for about a year and that she was at the house on East Sixth Street. Lawler asked if Velma directed Thomas or Jimmy Creighton where to drive when they left the house that night. He replied that she didn't say anything as Jimmy put her in the Thomas car along with their baby and Officer Wood.

"What is the disposition and temperament of Jimmy Creighton?" Lawler asked.

"Jimmy is pretty high strung and a man that likes to have his own way about things and Mrs. Creighton was more or less afraid of him and I imagine she would be afraid to rile him up," Thomas replied. When asked if Velma had seen any of the bank's stolen property, he told them that she hadn't. Thomas confirmed that he and the Creightons lived in the house for about thirty days and that he and Velma went by the name Hendricks. Also, a man named "Bill" was with them at the house on February 25, but Thomas didn't know his last name.

Under cross-examination by Schroeder, Thomas admitted that at about 10:00 a.m. that morning, there was a division made of around $27,000 on the dining room table, but Velma "had gone to the store" and hadn't seen the activity. When asked for a description of "Bill," Thomas said he wasn't as tall as he and had a dark complexion. During the shooting incident, "Bill," Jimmy and the three police officers were in the dining room, where the officers sat on the floor with towels draped over their heads. Thomas said that after they had stopped to tie Officer Wood to a telegraph pole, he told Velma to drive as he was suffering from the gunshot wound. During the drive to Belvidere, he handed Velma his pocketbook, which contained $1,700, and asked her to send it to his wife in Amarillo. When asked where the money came from, Thomas replied, "Sold liquor for it."

On October 19, 1931, Velma's trial began in district court with Judge Lewis H. Blackledge. The charge she faced was receiving $810 of the stolen bank money. County Attorney Schroeder recognized that it would be difficult to convict a woman and mother. He opened with: "The state's toughest obstacle in this case is the fact that the defendant is a woman." He retold the story of how she lived at the house with the bandits, was there during the gun fight and left with bandit Thomas and hostage Officer Wood. When caught, she continued to use an assumed name. He told the jury that money had been found sewn into her coat, in the baby's clothes and, remarkably, in the mattress of her city jail cell.

Attorney Apt opened for the defense. His argument centered on Velma's husband, an out-of-work barber and car salesman, who she'd known only three months before their marriage. Jimmy Creighton was known to have "an indomitable temper and at all times vigorously asserted authority over his wife." Mrs. Gates Corrigan of Shawnee, Oklahoma, testified as a character witness, as did Velma's mother.

During the second day of trial, bank cashier Herbert Nelson testified that the money recovered from Velma included old, larger-sized bills, some of which were Nebraska bank bills. At least one was marked "Nebraska National Bank of Hastings, Nebraska." John Bramble stated that on the way back to Hastings with Velma, she initially refused to reveal Officer Wood's location by saying she didn't know. William Foster, nearby neighbor to the bandit house, testified that he and his wife visited once when Velma introduced Thomas as "Mr. Hendricks."

Velma took the stand for over an hour. She told how she quit the tenth grade of high school and went to work at a five-and-dime store to help support the family after her father, Frank Meeks, passed away. She later worked as a telephone operator and, after three and a half years, was promoted to exchange superintendent. Her marriage to Jimmy Creighton was in 1928, and a year later, baby Bobby was born. Her husband was no longer employed as a barber or car salesman, and they began taking trips in search of a job. One trip was to Amarillo, Texas, where they met a man known as "Travis" (later known as Jim Thomas), followed by a trip to Detroit. After their return from Michigan, Velma said she was told to pack, and they came to Hastings, where a house had already been rented for them. Velma was told they were there "looking for a location for a drugstore." Jimmy told her to go by the name "Mrs. Hendricks" but refused to tell her why. Most of the time, Velma explained, Jimmy told her it was none of her business.

When Velma was asked about the money found with her, she said that after Thomas tied Wood to a telephone pole, she was instructed to drive, and he got in the back seat. She testified that she threw her coat back to him as he was sick from the wound, and *he* hid the money in the coat. She was asked why she kept the money, to which she replied, "It was a woman's instinct to preserve the money for the support of my baby." Throughout her testimony, Velma maintained that she knew nothing about the bank robbery and never saw the bank loot. County Attorney Schroeder declared that she "performed a despicable act of lending her condition of expectant motherhood to create an air of respectability at the bandit's East Sixth Street rendezvous." He said that it enabled her husband and Thomas to perpetrate the bank robbery that could not have been executed, as it was, without her help.

By noon on October 21, Judge Blackledge gave the jury their instructions. He said that to find a verdict of guilty, they must be convinced that the state has proven all four elements of the case: 1. That Mrs. Creighton received the currency described in the complaint; 2. That the currency was the property of the bank; 3. That she knew the that the money was stolen and that she accepted it with intent to defraud the bank; and 4. That the value of the property she accepted exceeded thirty-five dollars. Additionally, he told the jury that the crime she was charged with carried a one- to seven-year prison term if found guilty. However, their duty was to find guilt or innocence; fixing of the penalty was that of the judge. The *Hastings Tribune* described the trial testimony as "an intensely dramatic two hours that was crowded with all the elements of a blood and thunder novel. There was the sordidness of crime, the sensation of a gun battle and the halo of motherhood."

By 9:00 p.m. the following evening, after nearly thirty-four hours of deliberation, the jury was re-called to the courtroom. An astounding revelation was made by one of the jurors when he read a statement for the record. While examining Velma's coat during deliberations, a juror found an *additional* $200 hidden in the belt that had not been previously discovered. The jury vote was eight to four for acquittal before the money was found but changed to eight to four for conviction after the money was found. Unable to reach a final decision, Judge Blackledge declared a mistrial and set November 2 for a new trial.

The *Hastings Tribune* learned of another bizarre incident that added to the already strange case. A neighbor lady of the bandit house was entrusted by the owner with a key and was authorized to show the house to prospective renters. Prior to Velma's trial, the lady showed the house to "a relatively young man, neatly dressed," who said he was a bridegroom. After a walk through the house, the young man asked to see the basement. When told that there were no lights, he insisted and went down by himself. The following day, the owner of the bandit house discovered that a mattress that had been used by the bandits was missing. Nothing else in the furnished house was disturbed. He also found that one of the basement windows had been opened, apparently from someone inside the house. The incident had been reported to Chief of Police Dailey, but apparently thinking it was not important, he failed to record it in the police blotter or notify county officers.

Hastings' Rivoli theater manager Homer Garvin recognized what he saw as a true attraction and offered Velma Creighton a contract to appear in person. The *Tribune* read, "There's more than one path that leads to the stage," when they reported it. Velma rejected the offer, "in no uncertain terms."

Once again John Lawler petitioned the court to take the deposition of James Thomas, which took place at the penitentiary on October 27.

In an attempt to show intimidation of Velma by her husband, Jimmy Creighton, Lawler again asked Thomas about his disposition. Thomas explained, "He was very high tempered, overbearing at times. I will say that he is one of the highest strung boys I ever met in my life and he is subject to mad spells at times especially when crossed." When asked if he thought Creighton was dangerous to cross, he said, "I wouldn't care to cross him on the wrong side, I would be on the wrong side myself."

The subject of the bank loot in the bandit house came up again when Schroeder asked where it was counted. This time, Thomas said that Jimmie and "Bob" (the first time it was "Bill," and when called on this, he stuck with "Bill") counted the money on the bed in the west bedroom. Schroeder reminded him of what he told Chief Bramble two days after the robbery, when he asked, "You brought the money into the house, that you locked the doors, that you laid the money on the dining room table and began counting the money?" Thomas denied ever making the statement. Schroeder pressed Thomas again, saying, "Do you remember a visit made to you in the penitentiary by Renus Kargo, William Condit and Volcott Condit about March 8, 1931…when you told them that you, Jimmy Creighton and the third man counted the money on the dining room table and that the defendant [Velma] was in the room when the money was being counted and couldn't help but see it?" Thomas again denied he said that. Schroeder then asked if he remembered a visit by John Bramble, William Condit and Volcott Condit on April 18, 1931, where he had told them the same thing. Thomas denied the statement again. Thomas further denied the answers to questions that Schroeder told him he had made previously, including whether they drove around a while before returning to the house and about carrying the money into the house and counting it. Previously, his answers indicated that

Velma had driven to the store when they counted the $27,000 and returned an hour later. When asked about the money that he gave Velma while they drove south on Highway 81, Thomas stated that he brought the $1,700 from Texas.

Interestingly, the deposition consisted of only five and a half pages of Lawler's direct examination and forty-six pages of Schroeder's cross-examination.

The second trial of Velma Creighton began on November 2 in front of another packed courtroom. Most of that day was used for jury selection. Twenty-three witnesses would testify, recounting the incidents surrounding the bank robbery and Velma's presence at the bandit house. Chief Dailey testified that two newspapers shown to him by County Attorney Schroeder appeared to be the same ones found in the house on East Sixth Street. They both featured detailed articles about the robbery, which Schroeder maintained would confirm that Velma had to know of the crime. Chief Dailey and Officer Dryden both said that they found .32-caliber cartridges on the dresser in the Creightons' room. Dan Ricker, a juryman in the first trial, testified to his finding the $200 inside the belt of Velma's coat during deliberations. Thayer County sheriff Robert Geisler testified that when he and Deputy Baldwin arrested Velma at Belvidere, she told them that she didn't know where the man was who owned the coat, hat and revolver found in the car, that she had never been in Hastings and didn't know anything about the bank robbery. County Attorney Schroeder read the deposition of James Thomas and mentioned his changing stories.

Closing arguments were polar opposites, of course. The state declared that she was a criminal who aided in the bank robbery. According to the defense, she was an innocent victim. Her attorneys argued that she never sewed stolen money into her coat. She had merely pushed the cash into already existing holes in the coat, for taking care of her baby.

Velma again took the stand and gave the same information about herself as in the first trial. She added that she had read about the robbery in the newspaper but had no idea that her husband or Thomas had anything to do with it. She said that she never saw any weapons in the house. Regarding the night of the shooting, she said that when officers came to the house, she and Jimmy had gone to bed. Thomas occupied a bedroom on the other side of the house. Her husband had looked out of the bedroom door and then ordered her to dress quickly, telling her, "We're going to get out of here." She told the court that when the shooting started, she crawled under the bed with her baby. She again denied seeing any of the stolen bank money.

Attorney Apt asked her why she hadn't mentioned hiding the $200 that was found by the previous jury in the belt of her coat. "I didn't remember having put that money there, I only know that I stuffed money in every place I could find on the coat that would conceal it," she said. Apt then asked if she knew whether any money remained in the coat. "All I know is that there is still some money missing." Velma asked for the coat and searched it while the courtroom became very quiet. No further money was found.

An employee of Whisinand's store testified that he waited on Mrs. Creighton about 3:00 p.m. the afternoon of the robbery, but under cross-examination, he said he wasn't certain it was that day. Velma testified that she was at Whisinand's store during the hour that James Thomas said the money was counted.

On November 5, after four days of testimony, the defense rested. At 10:45 p.m., after eleven hours of deliberation, the jury reached a unanimous decision. It was sealed, and they were excused to go home to their beds. At 10:00 a.m. the next day, the jury returned and read the verdict: not guilty. Velma broke into tears, as did her friend Mrs. Corrigan. When Judge Blackledge excused the jury, Velma walked over to the jury box and shook each of their hands. She then approached County Attorney Schroeder and did likewise. A number of spectators approached her to shake hands, after which she sent a telegram to her mother in Nowata, Oklahoma, their new home.

At 2:00 p.m., the judge heard arguments on a defense motion to return the money and coat to Velma. Schroeder objected and explained that there were still two charges remaining against Mrs. Creighton and asked that the exhibits be retained. Attorney Apt argued that Mrs. Creighton had been duly charged with all of the counts filed against her, that the state elected at the outset as to which of those counts it desired to proceed and that the defendant had already been placed in jeopardy on all counts. The judge said the defense had agreed and read into the final record, "by their verdict, the jurymen fully discharged the defendant."

Schroeder told the court that he was well aware, with Velma's discharge, that the state had no further claim to the money. According to sworn testimony during the trial, only $350 belonged to her and the rest to Jim Thomas. Apt maintained that Mrs. Creighton was entrusted to deliver the money on Thomas's behalf, and whether or not she did that would not come under this criminal action but would rather be a civil matter between Thomas and Creighton.

Judge Blackledge agreed with the defense and issued an order for the return of the $810 found in Velma's coat and jail mattress, the $260 found in the baby's sweater, the $200 found in the belt of the coat and the coat itself. Court Reporter Lee Johnston then had Velma sign a receipt and handed her $1,270 and the infamous coat.

CHAPTER 8

A Startling Detective Story

Make 'em open the safe demselves, see?
—Ogden Standard Examiner, *April 12, 1931*

Most major bank robberies made the newspapers across the country, and Hastings was no exception. One notable report appeared in the *Ogden (UT) Standard-Examiner* on Sunday, April 12, 1931. The full-page article was captioned, "Here's a Dime Novel Thriller in Real Life—How Three Texas Bandits, a Mother and a Baby, Corralled Thirteen Bankers, Eleven Sleuths, and a Fortune in Loot." The article included the basics of the robbery, albeit partly written in a true dime novel style: "Stick up de bank guys when dey come in see?...Make 'em open the safe demselves, see?...De bulls will chase all over the state, see?...Den we move out wid de jack." A lavish layout of photographs included "Big Jim" Thomas, the Creightons, Officer Wood, Captain Yetman and the East Sixth Street bandit house. Not pictured was someone named "Brazo Bill," said to be bandit number three.

Detective magazines, sometimes referred to as "pulps," were extremely popular from the 1930s to the 1990s. Hastings mayor Joe Davis's son Leon was one of many Americans who devoured the sordid crime stories covered in each issue. They apparently bolstered his confidence in being able to find the hidden money in the bandit car.

Seven years after the great Hastings bank robbery, the crime was covered in one of these pulps. The article in *Startling Detective Adventures* magazine again brought the Hastings bank robbery into the national spotlight. The

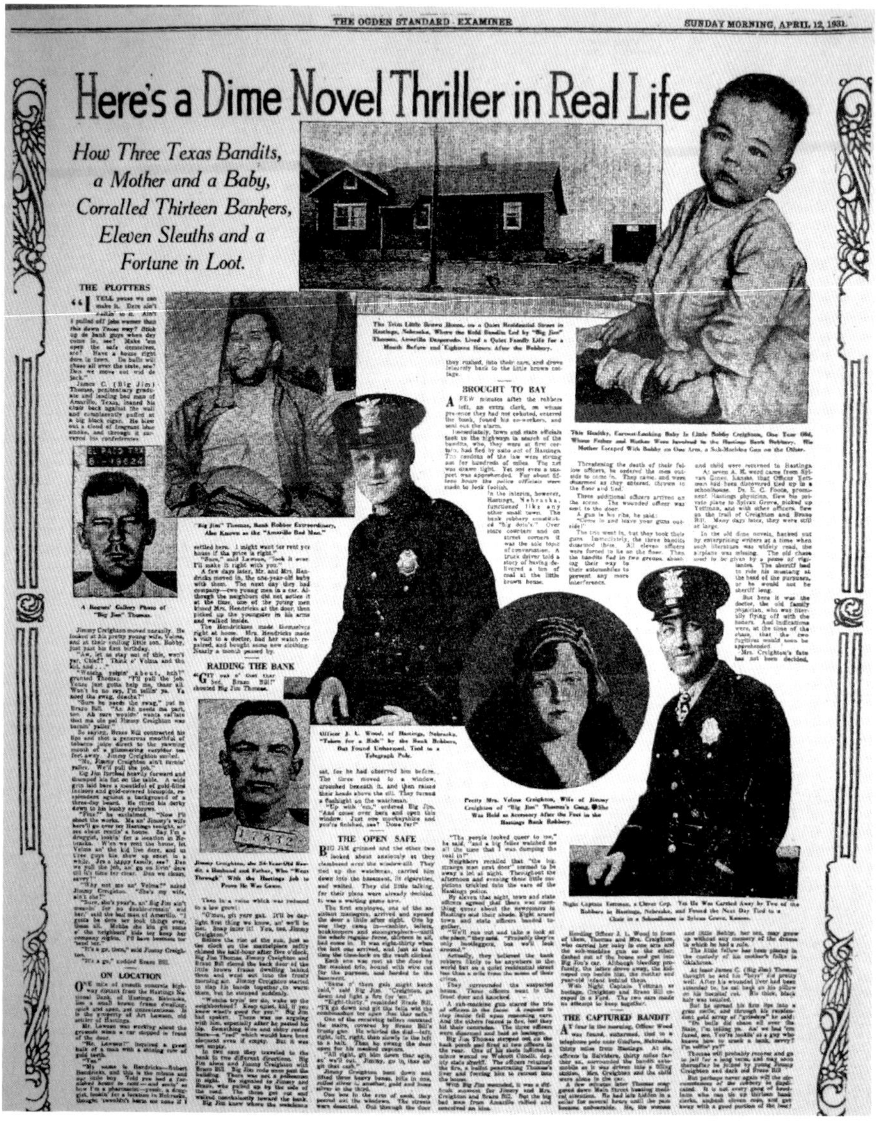

THE OGDEN STANDARD-EXAMINER — SUNDAY MORNING, APRIL 12, 1931

Here's a Dime Novel Thriller in Real Life

How Three Texas Bandits, a Mother and a Baby, Corralled Thirteen Bankers, Eleven Sleuths and a Fortune in Loot.

THE PLOTTERS

BROUGHT TO BAY

RAIDING THE BANK

THE OPEN SAFE

ON LOCATION

THE CAPTURED BANDIT

This full-page story of the Hastings bank robbery and shootout appeared in the *Ogden (UT) Standard Examiner* on Sunday, April 12, 1931. *Courtesy of the* Ogden Standard Examiner.

1938 issue featured an article by W.F. Yetman, police captain at the time of the robbery, as told to Jack DeWitt. It was titled, "Nebraska's Terrorists and the Kidnapped Sleuth." It's unknown who contacted whom to collaborate on the article, but true to the nature of these magazines, the information

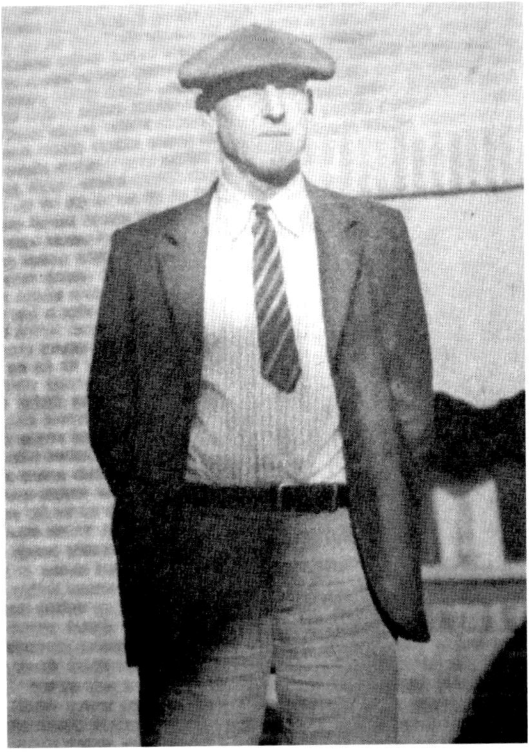

Hastings police captain Frank Yetman, shown here in civilian attire, collaborated with writer Jack DeWitt for a *Startling Detective Adventures* magazine article in 1938. *Author's collection.*

presented was full of name, place and other factual errors. Yetman himself may have mistaken some facts seven years after the event.

Jack DeWitt was a well-known crime writer. *Inside Detective* magazine said this about him in its July 1938 issue, "One of the most indefatigable writers in search of fact rather than fiction is Jack DeWitt."

Shortly after the 1934 killing of Public Enemy #1, John Dillinger, DeWitt received approval from Division of Investigation (later Federal Bureau of Investigation) director J. Edgar Hoover to interview Special Agent Sam Cowley. Cowley had led a special squad formed for the purpose of finding Dillinger. DeWitt's article about the division ran in *American Detective* magazine. A few short months later, Special Agent Cowley was killed in a gunfight with Lester "Baby Face" Nelson.

From the 1950s through the 1970s, Jack DeWitt was a screenwriter. In 1954, he worked with Wallace MacDonald on the film about death row inmate Caryl Chessman, the infamous "Red Light Bandit" of Los Angeles. The *Florence (AL) Times* described DeWitt as "an Arkansan who confessed to being a tramp newspaperman in earlier years. During the Depression, fiction wasn't selling so he turned out 2,500 stories, including an exposé of Devil's Island." DeWitt was quoted as saying, "This assignment [the Chessman film] is nothing new. I've witnessed seven hangings, two executions by gas, four or five electrocutions and several firing squads." DeWitt later wrote the screenplays for the hit films *A Man Called Horse* and *Return of a Man Called Horse*.

The *Omaha World-Herald's Magazine of the Midlands* of Sunday, September 30, 1973, featured a story about the Hastings robbery written by Harold Cowan. Titled, "Hastings Bank Robbery—A Script for the Keystone Kops," it was a light treatment of the case based on a small section of a county history book and interview with bank official Ivan Riley. The article mistakenly reported that Jimmy Creighton died after gouging his own eyes while a prison inmate in Missouri.

On the seventieth anniversary of the bank job, a 2001 edition of the *Hastings Tribune* ran an article on the crime that featured local resident Leon Davis. As a ten-year-old boy, he had helped to find the bank loot hidden inside the bandit's car.

Part II

CHAPTER 9

Jimmy Creighton, Coyne Hatten and Jeff City

I got a tough break.

—Jimmy Creighton, as reported in the Webb City Sentinel, *January 19, 1933*

More than two months passed after the Hastings bank robbery without any further suspect leads. Finally, in May, Jimmy Creighton surfaced. He was arrested in Joplin, Missouri, exactly one week after prison doors closed on Jim Thomas. Hastings authorities no doubt rejoiced as they contemplated his return to face bank robbery charges. Their excitement would dampen as they received details of the arrest.

About 11:00 p.m. on Saturday, May 16, Creighton (going by the alias "Jimmie Jones") and a lady friend, twenty-year-old Doris Adams, were drinking with ex-convict Mickey Carey and his wife. The Careys had an altercation, and Mrs. Carey's arm was cut by a bottle. The four drove from Joplin to nearby Webb City to have her arm dressed. They parked near the rear of the Morgan Drug Co. store at Webb and Daugherty Streets, which was a popular social gathering spot. Many people milled in and around the store on that Saturday night. The Careys went inside while Creighton and Adams stayed in the car for a few minutes. Doris was the first to step out, followed by Creighton. As the original story went, while stepping from the car to the sidewalk, Creighton bumped into local businessman Coyne Hatten, who took exception and asked him if he was looking for trouble. Creighton pulled out a .38 Colt revolver and fired three rounds point-blank into Hatten's chest. Hatten stumbled across the alley behind the drugstore

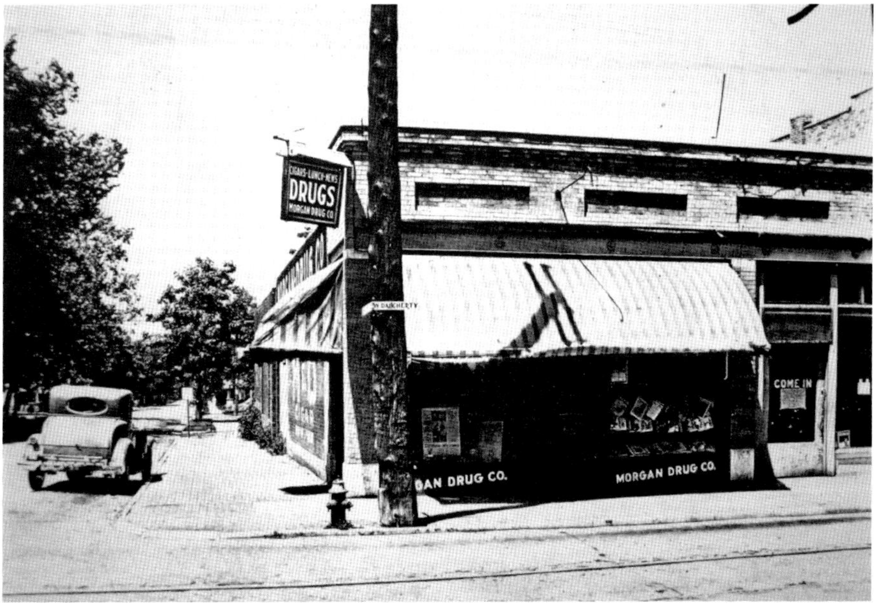

The Morgan Drug Co. store in Webb City, Missouri, in 1931. *Courtesy of the Webb City Area Genealogical Society.*

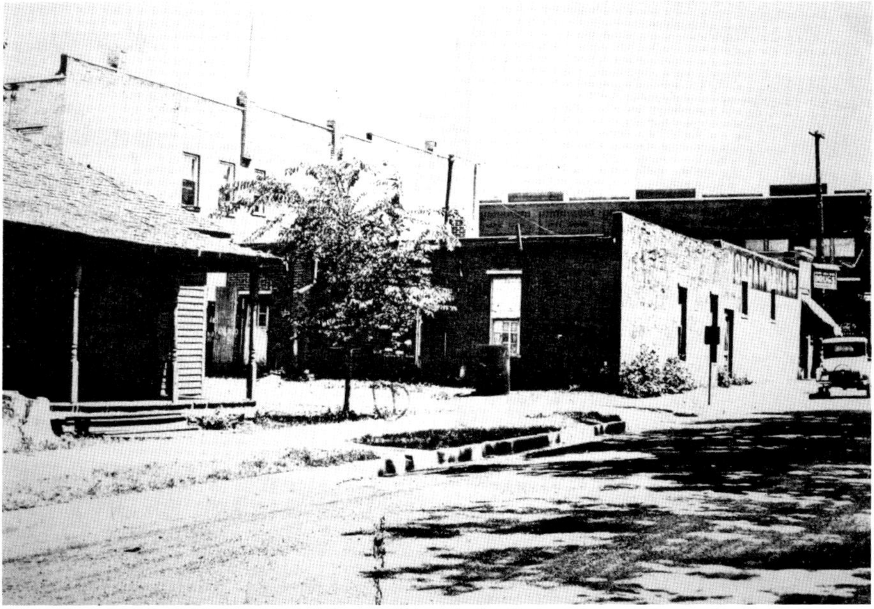

Rear of Morgan Drug Co. store where Coyne Hatten was shot by Jimmy Creighton. Hatten stumbled across the alley and fell dead by the small tree. *Courtesy of the Webb City Area Genealogical Society.*

and fell dead next to a small tree. At least four eyewitnesses saw Creighton shoot Hatten. Incredibly, Creighton then entered the drugstore and found the Careys, at which time they exited through the rear, got into their car and drove to Joplin.

About 9:30 the next morning, Joplin police detectives Ike Caylor and Len Vendeventer found Creighton in a stupefied state in his room at 708 Pearl Street. Creighton had lived at three different locations in Joplin, in one of which he roomed with Fred Barker of the Barker-Karpis gang. At the time of arrest, they found a fully loaded .38 Colt revolver, which had recently been fired, on the floor next to the bed and a sawed-off shotgun with a shoulder sling and ammunition inside a violin case. The detectives also found prescriptions issued to "Geers" from a South Coffeyville, Oklahoma drugstore, along with papers indicating that he had purchased a Dodge sedan in Coffeyville, Kansas, in March. They later learned that the car had been purchased in his name by the Tommy Hill gang of South Coffeyville, giving rise to suspicions that Creighton had ties to that gang as well. Creighton told the officers that the car had been stolen from him in Vinita, Oklahoma. About a week later, Tulsa, Oklahoma police notified them that they had just shot it out with Fred Barker and a man named Brown. The two escaped, leaving behind the car belonging to Jimmy Creighton.

When told he was under arrest for the murder of Coyne Hatten, Creighton said he was too drunk to remember what happened. He said, "If I shot him, I don't know anything about it, I was pretty tight."

Doris Adams was brought in and questioned. She told detectives that she had dated Jones (Creighton) three times and was with him Saturday night. When she and Creighton stepped out of the car near the rear of the drugstore, they met Hatten, whom she knew, walking north away from the store. She said hello and introduced him to her date. Creighton said, "I didn't get the name?" and Hatten replied, "That's all right, it doesn't make any difference." Doris said she had started off when she heard a shot and turned around in time to see Creighton shoot Hatten two more times. Hatten stumbled across the alley and fell dead.

Police reported the arrest of three Carthage youths who had words with Hatten in front of the drugstore shortly before the shooting. They were released Sunday morning when it was established that they had nothing to do with the murder.

The *Webb City Sentinel* touched on a theory about what may have actually been the cause of the shooting. They explained that possibly Creighton took it as a slight when Hatten wouldn't say his name. More importantly, the paper wrote, "Jones is supposedly to have been jealous of another man, a Webb City young man, like Coyne, wears glasses, and who is said to have been a friend of the Adams girl." According to local lore, Adams may or may not have been more than just friends with Hatten. At any rate, it would have been very easy for Creighton to be jealous of Coyne Hatten, a successful businessman at twenty-seven years of age with a wife and infant son. The son of wealthy capitalist Amos Davis Hatten, Coyne had graduated from the University of Notre Dame with a business degree.

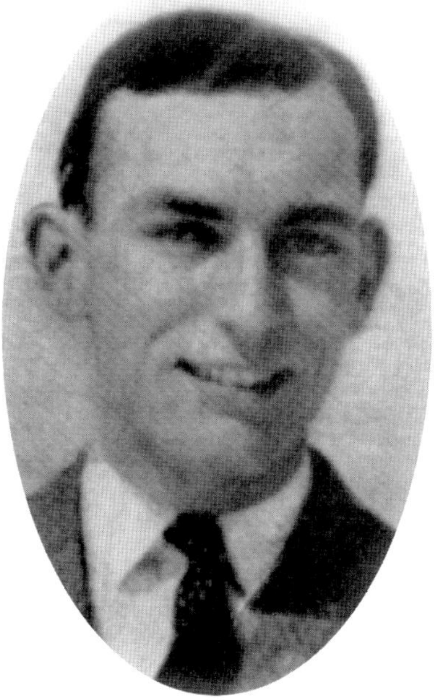

Coyne Hatten, son of Webb City industrialist A.D. Hatten, was twenty-seven years old when killed by Jimmy Creighton. *Courtesy of Deborah Hatten Lacey.*

Joplin chief of detectives Ed Portley believed that Creighton associated with Fred Barker, along with the Tommy Hill gang. He was also one of the last survivors of the old Matt Kimes gang. Additionally, U.S. postal inspectors identified Creighton's photo as one of the robbers of a post office in Borger, Texas, for $3,000 and another robbery near Amarillo for $13,000. (This was probably the Canyon bank robbery.)

Hastings authorities were relieved that Creighton had been captured but realized, with a first-degree murder charge, that chances of him being returned to Nebraska were nil. Adams County sheriff Ray Crosson sent a telegram to Joplin stating that he held a warrant for Creighton for bank robbery and other charges. The telegram ended with, "If you fail in your case we will take him."

Hastings authorities soon received more news from Joplin, not all of it good. The shotgun seized in Creighton's room belonged to the Hastings Police Department, as did, unfortunately, the murder weapon. The Colt Police Positive .38 used by Creighton to kill Hatten was the revolver taken from Police Chief Elbert Dailey (then sergeant) at the East Sixth Street house.

Velma Creighton's attorney Fred Apt arrived in Missouri to defend Jimmy Creighton, who was arraigned on May 21. He now admitted shooting Coyne

Hatten in self-defense and that he was assisted by "three other men" in the Hastings National Bank robbery. Apt said his client told him that he came to Joplin with $10,000 but had spent it all on gambling and drinking. Creighton offered to tell Hastings police the identity of a third bank robber if they would release Velma, then out on $1,500 bond. A deal was not reached. Officials witnessed Creighton sign over his automobile to his wife, telling his attorney that he wanted to see her properly defended. He also stated that she had nothing to do with the Hastings bank job.

The past was catching up with Jimmy Creighton. Canyon, Texas bank employees W.C. Black and Christine Upchurch arrived in Carthage, Missouri, where Creighton was jailed, and identified him as one of two men who robbed their bank of over $13,000 that past January. Like Nebraska, the chance of Texas having a stab at Creighton was slim.

On June 24, after a change of venue motion was overruled and jury selection completed, Jimmy Creighton's trial got underway in Carthage. He was defended by Fred Apt and T.C. Tadlock. Prosecutor Ray Watson presented Creighton's confession, which stated that he bumped into Coyne Hatten on the sidewalk near the rear of the Morgan Drug Co. store, at which time Hatten grabbed Creighton's coat and asked him if he was looking for trouble. Creighton said he then pulled out his revolver and shot Hatten, as he didn't like that treatment.

Witnesses testified that they heard a shot, turned and saw Hatten stepping back away from Creighton, who fired two subsequent shots. They said that Hatten stumbled across the sidewalk and fell near a small tree north of the alley behind the drugstore. An eyewitness, Pearl Meador, said that Creighton walked right by her as he went into the store after the shooting. She recognized him as she had met him previously at the drugstore.

Creighton took the stand on his own behalf and testified that Hatten threatened him because of the girl he was with, slapped him and made a move as if to reach for a weapon. He said he shot the man in self-defense. State's witnesses, however, testified that they heard no such quarrel. Worse yet, it was brought up by the prosecution that Creighton's confession contained nothing about the quarrel. His confession was read to the jury. It included some of his background and stated that he had served two terms in prison: a two-year term for burglary at the Granite, Oklahoma reformatory and a five-year term in the state prison at McAlester, Oklahoma, for car theft. He said that he had been discharged from prison on February 23, 1928, and came to Joplin from Bartlesville, Oklahoma, on April 27, 1931. He had stayed at three different rooming houses in Joplin.

Shortly before the shooting, Doris Adams told Creighton, "Hatten is all right. He has a wife and child." Creighton continued his confession saying, "I had been drinking all afternoon and I was under the influence of liquor. His conduct made me mad and I fired."

Detective Chief Ed Portley testified to a statement Creighton had made to him prior to making his written confession. Portley said he asked Creighton why he shot Hatten, and he replied, "I couldn't afford to be imposed upon by anyone. I was under cover for the Hastings Nebraska bank job, and I wouldn't stand for an arrest."

The jury was temporarily taken from the room while the defense argued against allowing testimony of Hastings police chief Elbert Dailey. He had identified the murder weapon as being the one taken from him while trying to arrest the bank robbers in Hastings. The defense contention was that the prosecution was only trying to make a stronger case by showing Creighton's past criminal record (as if his confession hadn't already done that). The judge overruled the objections, and Dailey was allowed to testify. During closing arguments, the defense attacked the prosecution for not placing Creighton's companion, Doris Adams, on the stand. Prosecutor Watson said that although she had been subpoenaed, the credibility of other state witnesses had not been attacked by the defense, and she added that "the state of Missouri has some regard for what witnesses it places on the stand."

The case was turned over to the jury after lunch on Friday, June 27. The large crowd waited in the courtroom, and Jimmy Creighton used the time to visit with his wife, Velma. Less than four hours later, the jury returned with a verdict of guilty. Creighton was then sentenced to hang. Jasper County deputy sheriff Clarence Scott handcuffed Creighton and led him into an anteroom before taking him to the county jail under heavy guard. Creighton was joking with the deputy and said, laughing, "You could have won some cigars off me if you had bet." At that moment, Coyne Hatten's wife, Helen, escorted by her father-in-law Amos Hatten, stepped in front of Creighton with upraised arms and tears running down her face, "How can I keep my hands off you?" she said, sobbing. The newspaper reported that Creighton was unmoved, and a second later, Mrs. Hatten was led from the room.

On the way to the jail, Creighton told his guards that he was glad the jury had sentenced him to hang, because he had a better chance for an appeal to the supreme court than if he had been given life in prison. "I expected to get life though. It's all right just so you don't shoot me," he told a jailor.

A motion for a new trial was quickly filed, and on July 2, Circuit Court Judge Harvey Davis overruled it and set a July 24 execution date. An appeal to the state supreme court was quickly filed. In the meantime, Jasper County sheriff Harry Stephens found a long knife in Creighton's cell, so he ordered five heavily armed deputies to transfer him and another death sentence prisoner to the Missouri State Penitentiary at Jefferson City for safekeeping. If the two men lost their appeals, they would have to be returned to Carthage, where the sentences would be carried out. Many counties still conducted their own executions at that time.

Creighton's wife, Velma, was still out on bond after the birth of their second child and visited him at the prison. In preparing for her own upcoming trial that fall in Nebraska, she asked her husband to give a deposition on her behalf. He refused.

Back in Hastings, the *Hastings Tribune* ran an article in the February 25, 1932 edition, on the one-year anniversary of the bank robbery. In addition to recounting details of the robbery, it reported the conviction of Jim Thomas, the acquittal of Velma and the death penalty facing Jimmy Creighton in Missouri. It reported that Jasper County officials feared mob violence.

The Missouri Supreme Court granted a new trial for Creighton in August 1932 and returned the case to Jasper County. (The judge was under guard because of anonymous threats made.) The court cited thirty-three errors, including not allowing a change of venue as the defendant was deprived of a fair trial due to bias and prejudice that existed in the county. The circuit court then granted a new trial to be held at Lamar, in Barton County.

On January 12, 1933, the new trial began after jury selection was completed. Barton County sheriff James Basset searched Jimmy and Velma Creighton, as he had been notified that Velma's sister, Mrs. Leo Allen of Nowata, Oklahoma, had purchased three files at a local variety store the previous day. He assigned three guards to watch Creighton.

Prosecutor Ray Watson advised Judge C.A. Hendricks that he again sought the death penalty. Twenty-seven witnesses were listed by the state. Testimony was given by eyewitnesses who said they observed no argument between the two men. Jimmy Creighton again took the stand and testified that Hatten had picked a fight with him, struck him and then reached to his right hip as if going for a weapon when he shot him.

The defense introduced Doris Adams as a surprise witness. She took the stand and testified that Coyne Hatten was quarrelsome that night and, in her opinion, intoxicated. She said that when she introduced the two men, Creighton did not hear his name and asked what it was. Hatten replied, "What's it to you?" She saw a quarrel was developing, so she walked away. She turned when she heard the first shot fired and saw Creighton fire twice more.

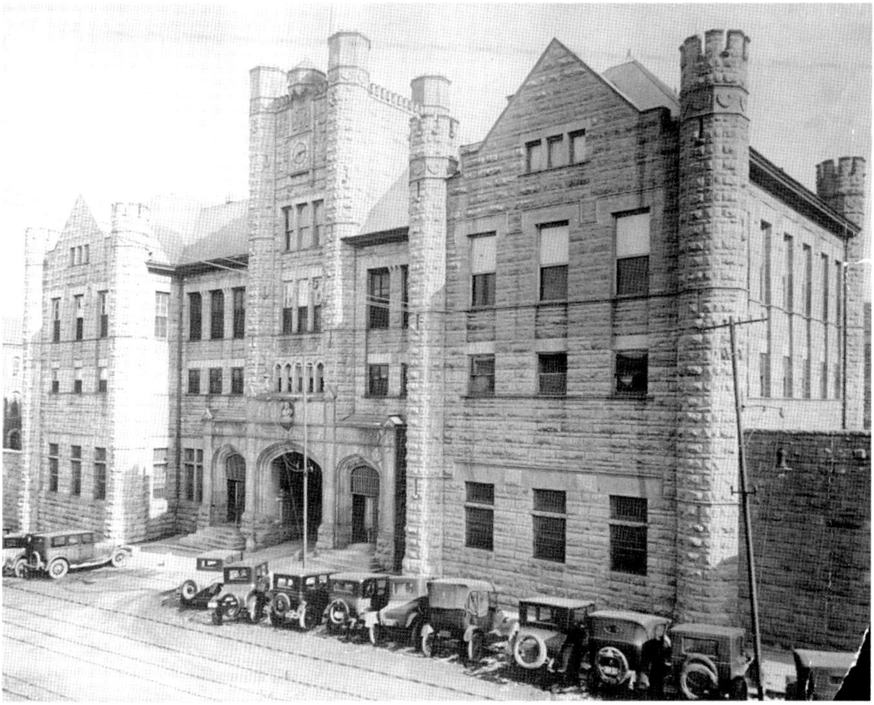

Missouri State Penitentiary, Jefferson City, as it would have looked to Jimmy Creighton upon his arrival to begin a life sentence for murder. *Author's collection.*

Judge Hendricks decided against a night session and took up closing arguments on Monday morning. The jury returned a verdict of guilty the following morning and set the penalty at life imprisonment. Creighton was quoted as saying, "I got a tough break, I shouldn't have received that much," and ordered his attorneys to again appeal the case.

That week it was reported that Creighton had come very close to the death penalty once again. Had it not been for a lone juror who balloted for a five-year sentence, the outcome would have been different. The other eleven, in order to compromise, agreed to life imprisonment instead of death. The prosecution regarded the life sentence as the result of one juror who opposed the death penalty, "although said juror did not so state when the jury was being selected."

After only a year in the Missouri State Penitentiary, James Creighton sharpened a fingernail file and used it to gouge his eyes. Moved to the prison hospital, officials believed that he would lose the sight in both eyes. Creighton believed that he would get a parole if he blinded himself. He apparently had been a model prisoner, even though he did attempt to escape while held at the prison for safekeeping before his trial.

Prison officials were somewhat skeptical, but Creighton continued to maintain his "blindness." His food was brought to him, he didn't have to work and fellow inmates wrote his letters and read to him. He was placed in a basement cell where he was joined by Luther Allen, another blind inmate, and his brother Walter in 1937. Walter was assigned to care for both men.

Eleven months later on April 30, 1938, Jimmy Creighton marched into Warden J.M. Sanders's office and declared that he had been able to see the whole time. His four years of blindness was a hoax. "When I jabbed my eyes with a file, I figured I'd win sympathy and a parole," Creighton told the warden. "But when you put that other blind man in the same cell with me, it wore me out." Creighton was put to work in the prison kitchen and later as a barber.

News of Creighton faded until July 8, 1944, when he escaped from Prison Farm No. 2. He was arrested in September 1945 in Texas on a robbery charge and subsequently returned to the Missouri penitentiary.

CHAPTER 10

Samuel O'Dell and Big Sky Country

All of you guys from Hastings?
—Samuel O'Dell, as reported by the Hastings Daily Tribune, *May 11, 1932*

While Velma Creighton prepared for her upcoming second trial and her husband waited in jail for the Missouri Supreme Court to grant him a new trial, bank robbers were busy in Big Sky Country.

On October 30, 1931, shortly after 2:00 p.m., two armed men entered the Custer State Bank of Custer, Montana. A third man, the driver, stayed in the car. They locked two bank officials in the vault and left with $1,500 in cash and $3,500 in Liberty Bonds. They were identified as the same men who robbed the Farmers State Bank at Worden of $2,000 only a month previously.

Yellowstone County sheriff E.M. Birely and Deputy Ed Penrod organized a search for the bandits' car, which was believed to have been a green Model A Ford with Wyoming license plates. Bank employees identified a photo of Samuel Lawson O'Dell as one of the robbers.

Not until March 1932 did arrests make the newspapers. Herman Hamilton and O.W. Crawford were arrested and lodged in the Yellowstone County jail for the Worden robbery. A third member of the gang, Walter Hayes, was picked up in Bartlesville, Oklahoma, about the same time.

In April, Sheriff Birely was notified that federal Prohibition agents had arrested a man named Jack Fanders in Sapulpa, Oklahoma, for transporting liquor. Inside the car they found three pistols, a sawed-off shotgun and a rifle. The man was identified as Samuel Lawson O'Dell, aka Jack Fanders (or Sanders), by the Oklahoma State Bureau of Identification.

Extradition proceedings began so O'Dell could be returned to Montana to face bank robbery charges. In addition to being identified by bank employees, he had been implicated by one of his cohorts who already occupied a jail cell in Billings, Montana. O'Dell, it was learned, had been indicted by federal authorities for violation of the Dyer Act (transporting a stolen auto across state lines) for stealing a car in Casper, Wyoming, only days before the Custer bank robbery.

Sheriff Birely received a telegram from the United States marshal's office in Tulsa that said there would be a delay in bringing O'Dell to Montana to face the bank robbery charges. There was an uncertainty whether the federal government would pay expenses to transport O'Dell. On May 4, Birely sent Deputy Penrod to Tulsa with extradition papers signed by Governor Erickson. After Penrod's arrival, the Oklahoma governor approved the extradition of O'Dell.

Two months earlier, Hastings police chief Elbert Dailey had received a "Wanted" flyer sent out from Yellowstone County. It featured O'Dell's photo and stated that he was wanted for the Custer, Montana bank robbery. He was described as being thirty-two years of age, five feet ten inches in height, 160 pounds with a medium build and with slate green or gray eyes, black hair, a scar near his left eye, thick lips and a medium complexion. It also stated that he had served a term in the Oklahoma State Penitentiary, where he was inmate number 17313. Dailey instantly recognized the wanted man as one of the bandits at the East Sixth Street house. He showed it to other officers who were involved, and they agreed that they'd seen him there as well. Dailey notified Montana authorities. When O'Dell was arrested, he was told that Deputy Penrod would be returning with the wanted man to Montana by train.

On May 10, 1932, officers met the train when it stopped in Grand Island, Nebraska. Chief Dailey, Patrolman Tommy Dryden and Sheriff Raymond Crosson from Hastings; Kearney County sheriff Renus Kargo and his deputy, Lars Johnson; and Minden police chief James Wood (who had been one of the kidnapped Hastings officers) filed into the passenger car where O'Dell was handcuffed and shackled. The *Hastings Daily Tribune* reported O'Dell's response to the officers: "'All you guys from Hastings?,' he asked sourly as they assembled before him." All six officers confirmed that O'Dell was the man they had seen, but O'Dell maintained his innocence regarding the Hastings bank robbery.

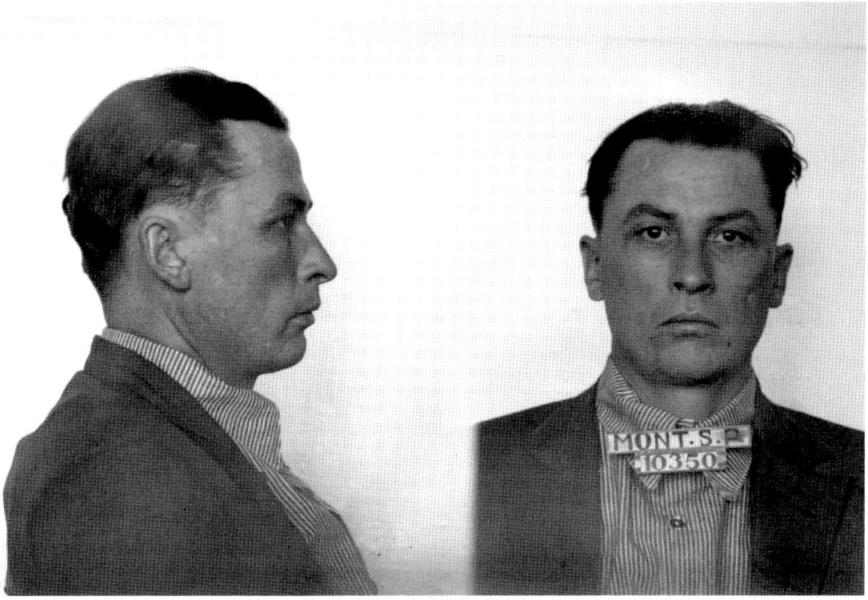

Montana State Prison mugshot of Samuel Lawson O'Dell in 1932 when he was incarcerated for bank robbery. *Courtesy of the Montana Historical Society Research Center.*

However, two days later, Adams County attorney Herman Schroeder filed a complaint in county court against O'Dell for bank robbery and kidnapping. This would pave the way to return O'Dell to face charges after he was released from Montana.

On May 17, O'Dell pleaded guilty to robbery of the Custer, Montana bank and was sentenced to ten years imprisonment. On May 24, 1932, he was transported with other convicted prisoners to the state penitentiary at Deer Lodge, Montana. His prison records described him as Samuel Lawson O'Dell, prisoner number 10350; born in Fort Gibson, Oklahoma; occupation, farmhand; age twenty-eight; five feet ten and a half inches tall; dark complexion; 183 pounds; brown eyes; black hair; had eighth grade education; able to read and write; and married to Alice O'Dell, of Claremore, Oklahoma. His Cherokee mother had died, but his father, John O'Dell, lived at Fort Gibson. He had an Indian chief tattoo on his right shoulder, and numerous scars were also listed.

O'Dell's arrest record began in 1927 with a term in the Oklahoma State Penitentiary for robbery. He was discharged a year before the Hastings bank robbery. His next arrest was in April 1932 for violation of the National

Prohibition Act in Oklahoma. Violation of the Dyer Act quickly followed, as did the bank robbery conviction in Montana.

On February 19, 1938, O'Dell was discharged from the Montana prison directly into the hands of Chief Deputy U.S. Marshal E. Lieberg to face the Dyer Act charges.

CHAPTER 11

Jim Clyde Thomas, Baxter Honey and Benny Binion

He's too dangerous to turn loose.
—*Sheriff Tom Abel,* Lubbock Morning Avalanche, *July 28, 1942*

James Thomas had served nine years and six months at the Nebraska penitentiary when he appeared before the state board of pardons on November 13, 1940. The hearing records indicated that he was forty-five years of age; born and raised in Waco, Texas; and had been married and divorced twice. He had two children by his first wife and three children by his second. He had a grade-school education and was formerly an interior decorator. He indicated that he had operated a drugstore and night club at Borger and a rooming house and dance hall near the Pantex munitions plant, both in Texas.

Thomas was asked many questions during the hearing. Many dealt with his family, prior arrests and, most particularly, the Hastings robbery. He was asked for the full name of "Bill," the third bandit. Thomas told them that Creighton had gone to Oklahoma to get Bill when Mills "backed out." (Mills, as one of Thomas's gang, had been arrested for the Canyon job.) He maintained that he never saw him before that. (In a statement made to the Condits in May 1931, Thomas said he and Creighton both went to Oklahoma to get Bill.)

William Condit said later in the hearing that when they interviewed Creighton in Missouri, he said he would tell them Bill's name if they dismissed charges against his wife. He added that Thomas also knew who

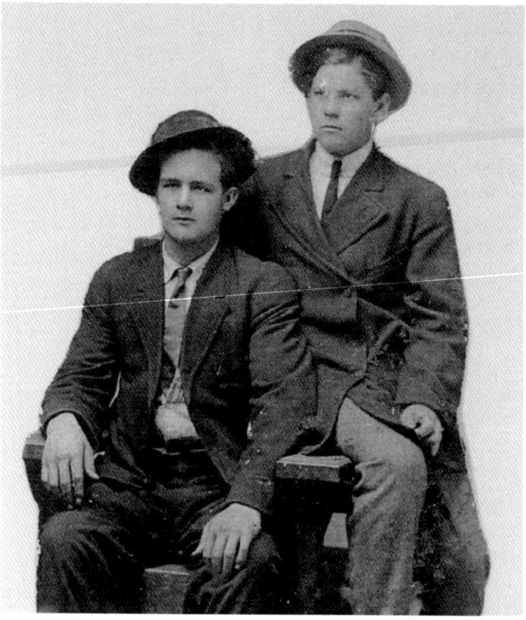

Jim Thomas (right) at about eighteen years of age. *Courtesy of Martha Williams.*

the man was. Condit told the board that he knew from experience that men who would attempt a bold robbery like Hastings "do not go into a job of that magnitude without knowing exactly who is with them. That would be absurd to even consider." Condit said that Creighton told him as much when he said, "Do you think you could go on a bank job with another fellow and be with him for several days and not know who he was?"

When asked about what happened inside their East Sixth Street house the night they took officers hostage, Thomas said, "Creighton had a machine gun and said we might as well kill them and used some cuss words. I insisted that he wouldn't do it, and he insisted he would. I knew Creighton wanted to kill someone, and I knew that he would have killed all those men. He did kill a man in Missouri after that."

Condit stated that at least forty rounds had been fired by the gang that night. He said that when the police chief, sheriff and another Hastings policeman drove up, they pulled up at the curb in front of the house, and "Creighton started shooting. He put eight .45 caliber bullet holes right through the house across the street. There was a piano in the room and the bullets hit a metal part of the piano and ricocheted off and hit the wall."

Volcott Condit also spoke at the hearing. Regarding Creighton he said, "To give you an idea of the type of man Thomas was with, about the first of March, he bought a brand new car and with Fred Barker, a bank robber you are familiar with, went to Oklahoma where they were to meet Alvin Karpis. After the meeting with Creighton driving, he noticed something wrong and jumped out of the car as it was going." Shots had been fired (presumably by the police) and Creighton's car was recovered with several bullet holes in the back.

Thomas's brother Wilburn explained during the commutation hearing that their mother was in her seventies. If Jim could be released, it would enable him to help with his eleven-year-old boy, who lived with their mother in Waco.

Amazingly, the board received twenty-two letters from Waco citizens indicating their support of a commuted sentence for Thomas. These included: bank officials, judges, district attorneys, county commissioners, a U.S. commissioner, the sheriff, a former police chief and others. Warren Montgomery of Waco promised to employ Thomas upon his release. Adams County, Nebraska sheriff Worthy Wood sent a letter neither recommending nor protesting his release. James Wood (ex-hostage officer) indicated that he had no objections to clemency.

Listed as unfavorable for release were his three arrests (prior to the bank robbery) and a statement county attorney Herman Schroeder made at time of commitment. William Hughes, secretary of the Nebraska Bankers Association, appeared and gave a statement that said, "It is not the conduct of a prisoner after his apprehension and conviction that should determine whether clemency should be extended, but the crime for which he was convicted."

William Condit closed his statement by saying, "It is true that Thomas has a likeable way, but that is true of a man who can commit such a serious crime, but so far as we know, his life for several years hasn't been spent along lines of regular employment."

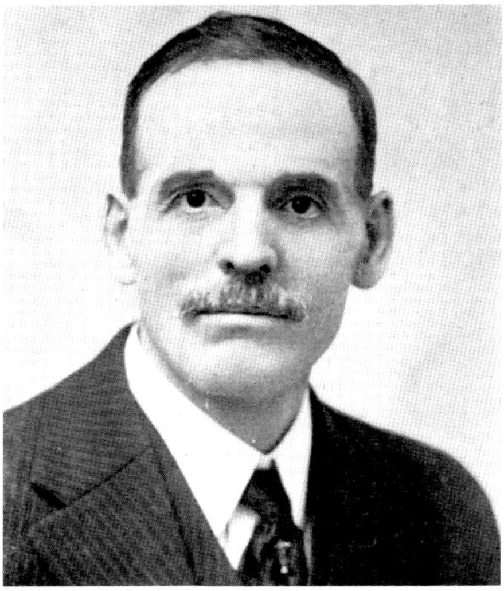

Former Nebraska state sheriff William C. Condit assisted with the bank robbery investigation. He and son Volcott were special officers of the Nebraska Bankers Association. *Author's collection.*

The only other letters of protest were from Hastings National Bank president Howard Pratt and Sheriff Worthy Wood, which were presented at Thomas's 1937 pardon hearing. The unfavorable section ended with, "Now wanted at Canyon, Texas."

Prison records indicated that Thomas had been a model prisoner and had accrued good time that included 118 "fire dept days" at the prison. Dr. Finkle stated for the record that Thomas was in the prison hospital for three months due to a gunshot wound in the liver, and he became well acquainted with him. He went on to say that when a hospital trustee position opened up, he asked Thomas to take the job, which he did. Dr. Finkle said, "It is a trusted place, a place where drugs could be sold if he wanted to sell them. He has been very faithful and very loyal." The records showed that his sentence would be served in full on May 8, 1956, or June 8, 1948, with good time.

Thomas was granted a commutation of sentence on Friday, December 13, 1940, and was discharged on the following Monday. His freedom was short-lived, however. A month later, Randall County, Texas sheriff M.E. Cantrell arrested Thomas in Waco, Texas, and took him to Canyon. He held a warrant for robbery of the First National Bank there in January 1931.

The Canyon story was similar to what happened in Hastings. Two men entered the home of an assistant cashier at 4:30 a.m. and then took him and his wife to the bank to wait for the time lock to release. They captured other bank employees as they came to work and bound them with wire. One unlucky hostage was then sheriff John Fry. The bandits wore masks and escaped the Canyon bank with $13,379. It was believed that there was a third member of the bandit group. Thomas's case was later dropped when witnesses failed to identify him. Memories had no doubt dimmed after nearly ten years.

Two years later, Jim Thomas was in the news again when he was arrested for assault with intent to kill. The incident happened about midnight on July 24, 1942, at the Maitland Jones farm north of Lubbock, Texas, when Thomas tried to kill Baxter Honey.

Honey, sixty-seven, a ex–Lubbock policeman and deputy sheriff, had been hired by Jones to guard his house and grounds. Honey later stated that he had observed a "heavy automobile" pull over on the Plainview–Lubbock highway about two hundred yards west of the Maitland farm on that rainy night. He heard a door slam and about fifteen minutes later saw a man walking across the grounds behind thick vegetation. He proceeded to a place where he could intercept the trespasser, and then shots were fired. The first bullet hit Honey in the leg as he pulled his own gun and started shooting back. When both shooters' guns were empty, the stranger emerged from the underbrush and hit Honey in the head, knocking him down. They resumed the bloody fight, pistol-whipping each other. At one point, the attacker limped away but apparently loaded one more cartridge into his gun, turned and fired. He missed Honey, and the fight commenced again. This time, Honey knocked his assailant to the ground with his pistol. Finally, the man stopped and walked off into the darkness. With great difficulty, Honey stumbled to the house, where Mrs. Jones called police at 12:45 a.m.

Because of his toughness, Honey suspected the intruder had been a soldier from the nearby South Plains Army Flying School, so military policemen were called and arrived first. Honey was taken into Lubbock by ambulance while military and civilian officers searched in vain for the attacker. They did find blood on weeds, a wire fence and on the driveway. Later they found a woman's stocking with eye slits and a hunter's cap in the nearby field.

About 6:00 a.m., the Joneses called the sheriff to report hearing a man "crying for help." Officers returned to the farm and found a wounded Jim Thomas laying in a field. They arrested him and transported him to the Lubbock hospital.

Both men were in shock when admitted to the hospital and immediately received blood transfusions. One bullet had struck Honey in the right thigh, and he suffered head wounds from the battering he took from Thomas's pistol. Thomas was hit in the right leg, and another bullet passed through his right thigh before emerging from the outside left thigh, crossing the buttocks.

No doubt as people read the news accounts they wondered what was behind the attack. Maitland Jones told reporters that he had been the object of intimidation recently by persons "living in Amarillo," and his dog had been poisoned sometime prior to the fight. He added that he believed the attack was an attempt to kidnap his wife. These revelations made it clear that the Joneses, and not Honey, were Thomas's primary target.

The two-hundred-pound Thomas was moved quickly to the hospital ward of the county jail. It was soon discovered that he was out on a $1,500 bond from a charge of robbing M.L. Young on December 23, 1941, one year after being released from the Nebraska penitentiary. His criminal record was recounted in newspapers, which included his FBI file number 245134. In addition to the earlier known arrests, a March 12, 1942 wanted fugitive arrest was made by the Texas Highway Patrol at Texarkana. Five days later, he was taken to Lubbock by Texas Rangers to face the robbery charge and had been allowed to post bond.

After the Honey attack, Sheriff Tom Abel threatened not to release Thomas, even if he did post bond, until the highest court forced him to do so. "He's too dangerous to turn loose," Abel declared.

In October, Jim Thomas was tried and convicted of assault with intent to murder Baxter Honey. His attorneys filed for a new trial, citing three "good and sufficient reasons," but the judge rejected the request. The ruling was appealed to the state Court of Criminal Appeals, but before there was a decision handed down, Thomas dropped the action. Finally, he was transported to Huntsville to begin his five-year sentence on the first of March. Interestingly, he listed "druggist" as his profession on the prison intake record. He also listed Waco as his home, instead of Amarillo, where he had lived at the time of the Hastings bank robbery. His second wife, Adelle, had divorced him.

By May, Thomas's leg wounds were causing genuine concern for his health. In fact, a prison physician said that without surgery, the prisoner would likely die in a few short months. On May 13, 1943, Thomas was given a sixty-day parole to have surgery in Galveston. Apparently, he preferred freedom over prison, because after surgery, he didn't return.

Thomas later surfaced in Dallas–Fort Worth, earning a degree of notoriety as an enforcer for the gambling underworld there. He sometimes worked for Dallas gambling boss "Cowboy" Benny Binion, as a guard for the illegal games.

By 1936, Binion controlled gambling in Dallas and had police, attorneys and other officials on his payroll, which assured no interference. His headquarters was the Southland Hotel, and he owned gambling concessions in several other locations. He would also get a percentage of the take from those games he didn't own outright. Failure to sign up for Binion's "protection" invited raids by police and confiscation of the competitor's equipment.

Sam Murray moved into Binion's territory and refused to pay for protection. He even foolishly attempted to take over Binion's numbers racket (Binion's personal favorite area) and ignored warnings. One morning in 1940, Murray completed his business at the Dallas National Bank and stepped outside. He normally had his bodyguard, Herbert Noble, at his side. But not this time. A top Binion associate by the name of Ivy Miller walked up and fired several shots at point-blank range, killing Murray. Miller was quickly arrested, but the message was clear. This was business as usual for the Cowboy. Over the past twenty years, Binion's arrests included attempted murder, bootlegging and gambling, but he spent very little time in jail.

Murray's absent bodyguard, Herbert Noble, was suspected of making the call that tipped off Binion that he would be at the bank unprotected. After Murray's death, seemingly as a reward, Noble took over gambling in several hotels and cafes, all financed by Binion. Noble paid Binion the normal 25 percent protection money. He became quite successful and purchased a large ranch north of Dallas. He built an airstrip and was also known for his aircraft repair and salvage business.

Ray Laudermilk, a respected high-ranking boss in Binion's gambling organization, married Sam Murray's widow, Sue. Through her urging, the couple approached Herbert Noble for help financing their own games. Noble agreed. Binion was very disappointed in Laudermilk and offered him a substantial raise, but he refused. Shortly after their last meeting, Laudermilk was found sitting in his car near a Dallas hotel. He had been shot six times with a .45 automatic. All six cartridge casings were found inside the car. Bob Minyard, a local tough who wanted to get Binion's attention and join his organization, thought killing Laudermilk was the answer. After borrowing a .45 pistol from a Binion deputy, he went for a ride with Laudermilk. After finishing the job, Minyard turned himself in for the murder, claiming self-defense. Although indicted, the case never went to trial.

If he didn't have enough reason to distrust Herbert Noble before, Binion surely did by then. Much to Noble's chagrin, Binion installed Bob Minyard as Noble's partner to keep a close eye on his operations. Binion also expanded his operations and power into Fort Worth.

Jim Thomas, still described as well dressed, polite and soft-spoken, was occasionally sent to deliver a warning for Benny Binion. His reputation preceded him, and it was generally thought wise not to ignore a suggestion from "Jim Clyde." At one point, even the Dallas police approached Binion and asked him to disassociate himself from Thomas. Binion may have removed him from the "public" work of guarding his games, but Jim Clyde remained available when the gambler chief needed him. Frank Cates, another dangerous gunman, was known to run with Thomas. The two men, as well as several others, were often listed as possible suspects during the periodic underworld killings in 1940s Dallas–Fort Worth.

Although the tit-for-tat killings would continue, the brutal murders of a doctor and his wife at Littlefield, Texas, would soon monopolize headlines.

CHAPTER 12

Jim Clyde, Dr. Hunt and the Texas Rangers

Mother and daddy are killed.
—five-year-old Jo Ann Hunt, Lubbock Morning Avalanche, *October 27, 1943*

A little before 8:00 a.m. on the morning of October 26, 1943, five-year-old Jo Ann Hunt carried her two-year-old sister Jane to a neighbor's home. Mrs. L.C. Grissom met the girls on that chilly morning as they approached in their nightclothes. Jo Ann's first words to her were, "Mother and daddy are killed—a bad man killed them." The girl was shivering and added, "The man poured water on me—I'm freezing." After putting the girls into bed, the Grissoms walked to the Hunt home.

The town of Littlefield, Texas, would never be the same after that fall morning in 1943. Thirty-seven miles northwest of Lubbock, the town of four thousand residents was home to a child by the name of Waylon Arnold Jennings, who would grow up to be a country music superstar. It was also the home of Dr. Roy E. Hunt, thirty-seven, and his wife, Mae, twenty-six.

When Lamb County sheriff Sam Hutson, a seasoned lawman, arrived shortly after 8:00 a.m. and walked into Dr. and Mrs. Hunt's bedroom, he was aghast. He whispered to himself, "Good God…it isn't possible." Before him in bed were the bound bodies of the Hunts, with "blood everywhere" as the *Lubbock Morning Avalanche* quoted. Dr. Hunt's face was covered with blood and had a gunshot wound at the upper bridge of his nose, made at very close range, as evidenced by the strong gunpowder residue visible. Mae

Hunt's head was also covered in blood. The cause of her death was blunt force trauma, presumably from a gun butt to the head.

Both bodies were bound with rope, heavy packing twine, a lamp cord (cut from a nearby lamp), neckties, a leather belt and a metal clothes hanger. Hangers torn from the closet rod littered the floor. The bindings cut into their wrists, throats and ankles. Their hands and feet were tied separately, and then the killer bound the Hunts closely together. So close in fact, that upon initial inspection of the crime scene, Mae Hunt was not immediately noticed.

Officers noted that the types of knots made were the same as those used on Mr. and Mrs. Lenro Keeton during a robbery at Lubbock in "March 1940." Either officials gave the wrong date of the Keeton robbery or a newspaper made a typo, but most Hunt articles that mentioned the Keeton robbery included this incorrect date. Of course, Jim Thomas, who was picked up and questioned in the robbery, would have still occupied a cell in the Nebraska penitentiary in March 1940. The actual date of the Keeton robbery was March 21, 1941, about three months after Thomas was released from prison. He was never charged. Besides using the same knots, the Keetons were anesthetized, as was suspected with the Hunts.

Sheer undergarments and a man's handkerchief were found under the Hunts' chins. These articles were not tied, which raised the possibility that they had been soaked with anesthetics. Officers did not detect any odors, but it was known that two anesthetics, vinyl ether and trityl-chloride, did not leave odors.

Sheriff Hutson spoke to little Jo Ann Hunt, who relayed her story. She said that she was awakened by a noise, got up and went into the kitchen, where she turned on a light and got a drink of water. She called out for her mother but got no response. She entered her parents' dark bedroom and saw a big man standing nearby. The man grabbed her by the shoulders and took her back into the children's room, opened a closet door, pushed her inside and "threw water on me from a can that smelled like gasoline and I went to sleep," she said. When she woke up, she went into her parents' room and found them. She told the sheriff that the man wore a mask with eye holes, gloves and a light hat, and he had hairy eyebrows and had "big ugly and round feet, in black shoes."

The killer had entered through a window in the children's room that had been left open after he fled. A small red, metal chair from inside the room was found outside the window. Apparently used as a step, it was slightly bent. A Lubbock policeman took plaster casts of footprints found outside the open window. Officers followed the footprints to a nearby alley, where they took tire impressions. A front tire of the suspect vehicle was identified as being a Lee brand tire. Texas Ranger Levi Duncan made a drawing of the Lee tire and meticulously measured every aspect of the tread.

Many people speculated about the murders. Were the victims tied up before they were killed? Were they killed before being bound? Was it a robbery or a narcotics addict looking for drugs?

Law enforcement officials and the district attorney felt from the start of the investigation that the killings were a professional murder-for-hire job. There was no evidence of a robbery or sexual assault. They deduced that Mae Hunt was awakened by the gunshot and struggled with the assailant. Evidence of a short struggle was observed: a cracked window, a damaged blind and the night light on the headboard was askew. She was then struck in the head, no doubt to silence her screaming. Thinking she was only unconscious, the killer bound them and securely tied her to her husband's body to prevent her from summoning help before he had escaped the area. The coroner indicated that Mae lived for about two hours after being struck.

The first step for the investigators was to find out where Dr. William Newton Jr. was at the time of the murders. Roy Hunt and William Newton Jr. had attended medical school in Galveston, with Newton graduating a year before Hunt. In the mid-1930s, both men served their internships at Jefferson Davis Hospital in Houston. During their internships, Dr. Newton met Ruth Nichols, a nursing student, and Dr. Hunt met her a short while later. Even though she dated both men, she kept it a secret from Newton. Since nursing students were not allowed to marry, Ruth secretly wed Dr. Newton but still loved Hunt, whom she possibly continued to see after the wedding.

Dr. Hunt met Mae Franks when she enrolled in nursing school. Mae quit the nursing program to marry Dr. Hunt in 1937. After graduation and internships, Dr. and Mrs. Newton moved to Cameron, and the Hunts set up their practice in Littlefield.

While the Hunts' marriage appeared to be a content one, the Newtons' was stormy. Ruth Newton separated from her husband, and by 1942, if not sooner, she was trying to contact Dr. Hunt. She apparently still loved Hunt and wanted to try to get back together with him. The possibility exists that she told her husband she had been seeing both men, even after their wedding. This understandably could have contributed to a rough relationship.

On the evening of May 20, 1942, the Hunts were entertaining several friends at their Littlefield home. During the evening, Ruth called three different times asking for Dr. Hunt to meet her. He refused. The last call was made from a local gas station after midnight. He finally told his wife and company who was on the phone and left to meet her about two and half miles east of town. He stopped his car near Ruth's on a dark stretch of road and walked up to her door. Dr. Newton appeared behind him and told Hunt that Ruth was a married woman. He then shot Dr. Hunt twice in the torso with a .38 revolver. Hunt ran into a nearby field as Newton fired more shots at him. The Newtons finally gave up trying to find Hunt and drove away. Dr. Hunt was able to drive himself back into Littlefield, to his own hospital, where he underwent emergency surgery.

The Newtons were quickly arrested and jailed. That fall, Dr. Newton was convicted and sentenced to seven years. He immediately appealed and posted bond. Ruth Newton was also out on bond, awaiting her trial. It was believed that the reason Ruth Newton was part of the murder plot on that lonely stretch of road was that Dr. Hunt refused to rekindle their relationship.

Officers questioned the Newtons, who were both still out on bond for the attempted murder of Dr. Hunt the previous year, and established that they were home in Cameron (418 miles southeast of Littlefield) on the night of the Hunt murders. They claimed to have never heard of Jim Thomas. Meanwhile, a reward of several thousand dollars was raised by citizens in Littlefield for capture of the killer.

With little to go on, Texas Ranger Captain Manny Gault joined Sheriff Hutson in the Hunt murder investigation. Gault had been one of the lawmen with Frank Hamer who unceremoniously ended the crime spree of Clyde Barrow and Bonnie Parker near Gibsland, Louisiana, in 1934.

The night after the murders, Jim Thomas was arrested as a parole violator in a Galveston hotel, where he was registered under an assumed name. Texas Rangers transported him directly to Lubbock for questioning. When booked, he had $101.48, an expensive bag, a wristwatch, a pencil set, a few snapshots and a greeting card signed in large capital letters from a female child. They attempted to retrace his movements since May 13, when he was given parole to have surgery on his leg wound. Nothing of value was learned from Thomas, which didn't surprise anyone. Officers commented that he'd been their prisoner before. Good police work and a tip from known Thomas associate Lon Holley had led to the arrest. Unfortunately, Holley's name was leaked, and it appeared in the newspapers.

With no worries about Thomas posting bond, the officers fanned out across the state to establish his whereabouts the week of the murders. They interviewed many people known to associate with Thomas.

Thomas was finally convinced to make a written statement, which he refused to sign. The statement made to the Rangers indicated that he did leave Galveston several days before the Hunt murders and went to Amarillo to see "a married woman," whose name he wouldn't reveal. (Amarillo, in the northwest part of the state, is about 660 miles from Galveston on the southeast Gulf Coast.) He said that he stayed part of the time with friends in Amarillo (118 miles northeast of Littlefield) and in fact, borrowed their car the evening of the twenty-fifth to spend time with his secret lady friend. He stated that he didn't leave her home until 1:30 a.m. and spent the night sleeping in the car. No witnesses could verify that. He denied having been in Littlefield during the visit to his friend.

Sheriff Hutson verified a phone call Thomas made from Amarillo to his female Galveston friend on the morning of the twenty-sixth, telling her that he was with a married woman (during the time of the murders). The sheriff believed this was done to establish an alibi. Officers also knew that Thomas had worked in the Nebraska penitentiary hospital and there became familiar with anesthetics. Also, Thomas had been identified by Littlefield café owner Eddie Glass. He stated that Thomas had been in his cafe for supper on both Sunday, October 24, and Monday, October 25 (the evening prior to the murders). Glass said he didn't know who Thomas was but remembered him well. He described him as having a slight limp and wearing work clothes. Glass added that he stared at Thomas because something about his eyes attracted his attention.

Thomas had stayed with friends, Mr. and Mrs. Sid Veazey, while in Amarillo. Veazey, who operated a garage and filling station that was located behind his house, reported that Thomas borrowed his 1939 Plymouth sedan on Sunday, October 24, returning about 11:00 p.m. Officers found a piece of packing twine on a burner inside a heating stove in the garage that had severed ends and matched the twine used to bind the Hunts. They also seized a pair of basketball shoes belonging to Veazey's son, Alvis, that appeared to match the footprints found. Evidence that the rubber soles had been buffed to remove some features of the tread was observed. Two buffers used in tire repair were present in the garage. Alvis had worn the shoes on Friday, October 22, but had left them in his closet when he, his father and friend Buck Holden left that Monday morning (the day before the Hunt murders) for a deer hunting trip to Gunnison, Colorado.

Texas Rangers found Thomas's friend Red Craig at his Amarillo home and the 1942 Oldsmobile that he had loaned to Thomas on Monday, October 25. The car was impounded after a Lee tire was observed on the front. Body damage matched the height of some broken concrete blocks found in the alley near the Hunt home. Craig would later testify that the car had body damage when he loaned it to Thomas but was damaged worse, in the same spot, after it was returned. Craig also told the Rangers that he (Craig) had thrown a gun into the river, because he was afraid it might have been evidence. Even after excavations rerouted the river's flow, the gun was not found.

In the spring of 1944, Jim Thomas was indicted for the murder of Dr. Roy Hunt. He was not charged in Mae Hunt's death. The indictment alleged that "Jim Thomas on or about the 26th day of October, 1943, in the county of Lamb, and State of Texas, did then and there voluntarily and with malice aforethought, kill Roy Hunt by shooting him with a gun." Part of the testimony included Texas Department of Public Safety crime lab experts who said that the casts taken of footprints outside the Hunt home matched the seized basketball shoes in every measurement, differing only in parts of the tread design that were missing on the shoes themselves. On August 30, at the end of his trial in Plainview, Thomas was found guilty and sentenced to die in the electric chair. An appeal was filed, and a new trial was granted due to misconduct in the jury room (they had discussed his prison record).

The second trial began on November 27, where a change of venue to Lamesa was granted. In January 1945, he was found guilty once again and sentenced to death, and once again an appeal and new trial were granted. An appeals court reversed his conviction, citing circumstantial evidence in that trial was not sufficient to justify the death penalty. A third trial at Sweetwater resulted in a sentence of life imprisonment.

On June 28, 1947, the Texas Court of Criminal Appeals made decisions in two related cases. First, they reversed Jim Thomas's third conviction, ruling that evidence was insufficient to establish guilt. He was released from jail after being allowed to post a $6,000 bond while preparations began for a fourth trial.

The other court of appeals decision was the affirmation of the conviction and two-year prison sentence handed down to Dr. William Newton for his 1942 attempted murder of Dr. Roy Hunt. With Dr. Hunt dead, the star witness against Newton, the case stumbled through two more trials before he was finally convicted. Dr. Hunt's testimony from the original trial was used as evidence in the subsequent proceedings. Newton spent only eleven months of a two-year sentence in prison.

Jim Thomas had five attorneys defending him in the Hunt murder case. Dr. Newton had six attorneys to defend him in the 1942 attempt on Dr. Hunt's life. Speculation was rampant as to how they could afford such legal extravagances. It was believed that Dr. Newton (along with other area doctors) was involved in an illicit drug ring, but he was never prosecuted. This might, however, explain how Dr. Newton could afford a hit man and all of his legal expenses.

Officers in the small town of Rosebud, Texas (forty miles south of Waco, Thomas's hometown), were alerted to a bank robbery on November 14, 1947. The night watchman of the First National Bank was taken by two large, unmasked men to a nearby barn and tied up. A side door of the bank was forced open, and all fifty-two of the safety deposit boxes were pried open. It was feared that the loss would reach $100,000. The main vault was not disturbed.

By early 1948, Jim Thomas was living in Fort Worth. He bought a house at 2117 Hillcrest from defense attorney Byron Matthews. A new, two-tone Cadillac sedan soon occupied the driveway. Newspapers described the

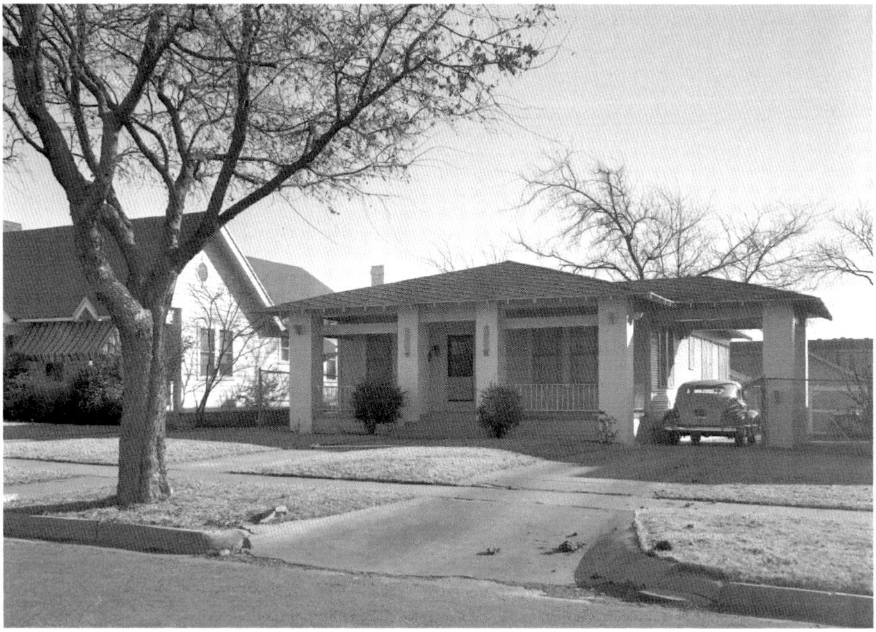

Jim Clyde Thomas's Fort Worth home at 2117 Hillcrest about 1950. The house and late model Cadillac in the carport showed that he was doing well. *Courtesy Fort Worth Star-Telegram Collection, Special Collections, the University of Texas at Arlington Library, Arlington, Texas.*

area as "a swank residential district...in Arlington Heights, considered one of the finer residential sections."

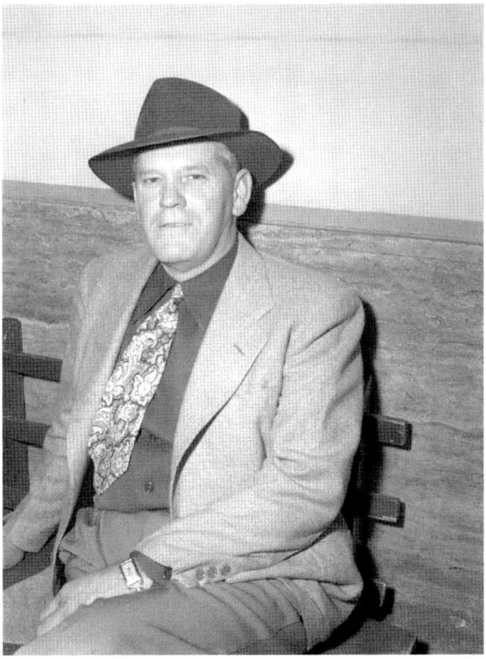

Jim Clyde Thomas waiting to be questioned in the murder of Lon Holley. *Courtesy Fort Worth Star-Telegram Collection, Special Collections, the University of Texas at Arlington Library, Arlington, Texas.*

The papers were once again writing about Thomas, this time about being questioned by Fort Worth police in the murder of Lon Holley. Another underworld figure, Holley was the man who tipped off Texas Rangers regarding the suspected involvement of Jim Thomas in the Hunt murders. During the late evening of March 6, 1948, Holley had received a phone call. He wrote the names Frank Cates and Jim Thomas on a note and gave it to his wife before leaving. He told her that if he didn't return, she'd know something happened. He was found the next morning behind the wheel of his car. Holley had been shot twice in the back of the head, and the side window and windshield before him were shattered. Authorities believed he was killed to keep him quiet. They reasoned that Holley had information about the Rosebud bank robbery (for which Thomas and Cates were suspected) as well as the Hunt murders. The .38 revolver found on Holley's hip was first thought to be the Hunt murder weapon, but this was later proved false. During questioning, Thomas told police in his normal, calm, polite way, "No, I didn't do it. I wouldn't shoot anybody. Why, human life is a flowering bud to me. I wouldn't crush it." Frank Cates was also questioned, but afterward both he and Thomas were released for lack of evidence. Holley's name was added to the growing list of unsolved murders in which Jim Thomas was suspected.

CHAPTER 13

Jim Clyde and "The Cat"

"It's just a matter of time."
—Herbert Noble, Life *magazine, May 14, 1951*

By 1946, tensions between Benny Binion and Herbert Noble reached the breaking point. Binion suspected that he was not getting his full 25 percent take from Noble's operation. He sent word to Noble that one of his men would personally supervise every count in the future. Noble, still angry with his forced partnership with Bob Minyard, told Binion he would count his own money. This was not what the gambling boss wanted to hear, so he decided to raise the cut from Noble to 40 percent. Predictably, Noble was enraged and told Binion "where to go." During the second week of January, a deputy sheriff stopped by Noble's Dallas Airmen's Club and told him to shut down his illegal gambling. Noble refused.

In the early morning hours of January 12, Noble locked up for the night and headed home to his wife and daughter. He immediately noticed a Cadillac following him. After several detours, the Cadillac still followed. Noble decided to head away from his family and on to his ranch north of the city. Noble's Mercury was no match for the Cadillac at high speed on the open road. The pursuer got close, and the passenger opened fire with a shotgun that shattered Noble's rear window. Several rounds of a .45 left holes in his trunk lid. Noble was unhurt in the shooting but lost control of the car, slid into a ditch and ran toward a farm house. The two men in the Cadillac got out and fired several shots at Noble, one hitting him in the back.

He was able to take cover as the awakened farmer turned on lights to see what was going on. The two men drove away.

From his hospital bed, Noble told deputies what had happened and identified Johnny Grisaffi and Lois (pronounced "Loyce") Green, two career criminals, as his attackers. He didn't name the person who had sent them and added that he wouldn't press charges. The battle was on, however.

Only two days later, Bob Minyard was shot to death in his driveway by two gunmen. Even though no arrests were made, Benny Binion knew who had killed his man. Binion had more problems to contend with that year. Through elections and resignations, his bought-and-paid-for sheriff's department, police department and prosecutor's offices had changed leaders. The new government officials moved to rid Dallas of illegal gambling, and that included Benny Binion. Herbert Noble even made sizeable campaign contributions in hopes of replacing Binion. The Cowboy assumed that all the contributions had been skimmed off his own take by Noble.

By spring, the new county prosecutor had started after gamblers in earnest. Binion thought it was a good time to turn over management to trusted partners and move to Las Vegas. He arrived in time to attend the grand opening of Ben "Bugsy" Siegel's Flamingo Club. The operation was backed by the New York mob. Binion became a partner in the Las Vegas Club downtown and was the man who originated "comps," or free food and drinks, for gambling customers. Although fellow casino owners didn't appreciate his inventiveness, the idea caught on and is still in use today.

Two years later, on May 20, 1948, Herbert Noble slowed his car for a cattle guard at his ranch. A shotgun was fired from cover, and buckshot struck his arm. A neighbor took him to the hospital, where he claimed that he'd accidentally shot himself, but deputies learned from his wife, Mildred, what had happened. Authorities later suspected Lois Green as the shooter in another attempt to fill a contract on Noble's life.

While working in his office at the Dallas Airman's Club on Valentines Day in 1949, Noble was alerted by a customer that a man had been crawling around underneath Noble's Mercury parked on the street. Police discovered blasting caps and several sticks of dynamite wired to the starter of his car. This was the third attempt on Noble's life. Even though Benny Binion had moved to Las Vegas, bygones would not be bygones.

Binion was indicted on gambling charges in Dallas, but his Nevada attorney helped him avoid extradition. The Cowboy bought the El Dorado Club in Las Vegas and renamed it the Horseshoe Club. The new downtown casino became famous. A popular feature was $1 million mounted behind bulletproof glass where thousands had their pictures taken.

Meanwhile, Herbert Noble began carrying an M-1 carbine with him. On September 7, 1949, he noticed a strange car driving by his ranch, so he gave chase. He'd heard through the grapevine that the contract on his life was worth anywhere from $5,000 to $50,000, but no one knew for sure. The suspicious car lost control on a curve and rolled. Three gunmen got out and fired at Noble, hitting him in the leg. Jack Nesbit, a known explosives man and a cohort of Frank Cates, was arrested for the assault but never indicted. Police believed that Cates and Jim Clyde Thomas were the other two shooters.

On November 5, 1949, Noble left his Dallas home for a business appointment. Instead of taking his Mercury, he drove Mildred's Cadillac. The last thing Mildred would do in her thirty-six years of life would be to turn the ignition key of the Mercury. The explosion was heard for miles. All that remained of the car was the smoking chassis. The body of Noble's wife was found close by. Retribution was swift. On Christmas Eve, newspapers reported that Lois Green was taken to Parkland Hospital, where he died of buckshot wounds.

On New Years Eve, as Noble stepped out of his Dallas home, gunfire erupted. Seriously wounded in the arm and side, he was able to crawl back inside the house. This sixth attempt on his life landed him back in Methodist Hospital. Noble told police that the shots were fired from a car parked in the street, but he couldn't identify the two men inside.

Still hospitalized on February 7, 1950, Noble turned on a lamp and got out of bed. A sniper's bullet came through the window and hit the ceiling, forcing him to dive for the floor. He had narrowly escaped death again. At some point, Dallas County sheriff Bill Decker gave Noble the nickname "The Cat."

Attempt number seven came on June 14 at a county road intersection near Noble's ranch. As he slowed for the turn, three loads of buckshot were fired from cover, blowing out a tire. Noble later posed for a photo beside his new Ford, showing the holes in the front fender and driver's door. Franklin Strong and Leroy Goss were suspected. The contract on "The Cat's" life was common knowledge by then, and it attracted many interested parties.

With Benny Binion in Las Vegas, more attempts were made to take over his Dallas–Fort Worth gambling interests. Nelson Harris let it be known that he would be the next gambling boss. Someone sent Jim Clyde Thomas to give him some friendly advice, which he rejected. On November 22, 1950,

Harris and his pregnant wife were killed when their car exploded. A list of "usual" suspects were rounded up for questioning by the Fort Worth police. At the top of the list was fifty-five-year-old Thomas, who was picked up by police at his home on Hillcrest. Other suspects questioned included Jack Nesbit, Frank Cates, Carl Hall, George Wilderspin and Grady and Robert Whitehead. No arrests were made in the killings.

The ninth and tenth attempts on Herbert Noble's life involved his airplane engines. One of these exploded when he attempted to start the plane. A heavy shield between the engine and cabin saved his life. A cylinder on the replacement engine was found to be packed with nitroglycerin gel.

Just before noon on August 7, 1951, Noble drove his brand-new Ford down the ranch road and pulled up next to his mailbox. His killers were the only witnesses to the explosion that lifted the Ford into the air and dropped it upside down on the road. "The Cat" had used up all of his lives. It was over an hour before a neighbor came down the road and found the wreckage.

The blast made a crater in the road four feet deep and five feet across. Parts of Noble's body and the car were scattered two hundred yards in every direction. The upper torso was intact enough that Texas Ranger Lewis Rigler could identify the forty-two-year-old Noble.

Benny Binion, smarting from a series of raids on his Dallas gambling establishments and facing additional indictments, had been informed of Noble's death by friends. When reporters asked for his reaction, Binion told them he didn't have any feeling about it. He added that he didn't have anything to do with the deaths of Noble or his wife.

Life magazine reported on each of the ten attempts to kill Herbert Noble in its May 14, 1951 issue; photos of Noble and the locations of each attempt were included. The August 20 copy featured a full page on his violent death. A large photo of the grisly scene showed the wreckage of Noble's 1951 Ford.

Officers interviewed the postman, who had skipped Noble's mailbox that day as he had no mail to deliver. He said that he'd seen a blue pickup parked behind some trees about a quarter mile away from the scene but hadn't thought anything about it at the time. Another witness had seen an automobile with two men parked near a bridge not far from Noble's ranch. When the witness approached, the two men hurriedly closed the hood and trunk lid, got inside and drove off. Their identities could not be verified.

CHAPTER 14

Texas Badman Forgets His Gun

...one of the most cold blooded triggermen...
—Fort Worth police, as reported by the Waco Times-Herald,
August 23, 1951

Texas Ranger Lewis Rigler was placed in charge of the Herbert Noble investigation. Detective Lieutenant George Butler of the Dallas police worked alongside him. As the case proceeded, police indicated that they had good reason to search for three men in Fort Worth. Newspapers reported that one of these men "was once arrested for assault to murder Noble, but was never tried." They were obviously referring to Jack Nesbit, Frank Cates and Jim Clyde Thomas. Officers recalled that in September 1949, Noble had chased a suspicious car near his ranch. A gun battle had ensued after the car rolled and three men got out shooting. Nesbit had been the only one arrested. The suspect list would grow.

The investigation revealed that Jim Thomas owned interests in clubs and tourist courts in Odessa and Snyder and the Dragon Grill, ten miles west of Midland, Texas, possibly financed by Benny Binion. When questioned as to his whereabouts at the time Noble was killed, Thomas said he and his wife, Mary, had gone to their traveler's courts in Odessa, arriving on August 6 and checking out on the eighth. Noble was killed on August 7. Thomas's presence for that time period was in question, however. No one saw him there at all on the seventh. That particular day, Mary took her husband's new Cadillac to visit friends in Odessa.

From Fort Worth policemen, detectives found out that Thomas had been driving a blue pickup when he was stopped and cited for a minor violation. Through informants, who refused to testify, the officers learned that Finley Donica owned a pickup like that seen near the Noble ranch. Donica had been one of a group of three men who stopped into a cafe in Lewisburg for lunch (within an hour of the explosion) in a blue pickup. The town was not far from the Noble ranch. J.R. Gilreath and Bob Braggins were two more underworld types that they learned were associated with Donica.

Rigler and Butler were compiling more and more circumstantial evidence which included the four men, but it was not enough for arrest warrants. Informants were talking but were rightfully too scared to testify.

On Wednesday, August 22, 1951, Jim Clyde Thomas left his home on Hillcrest and headed north toward the small town of Durant, Oklahoma. The purpose of the two-hour drive was to see his longtime business associate, Hubert Deere. The two had reportedly partnered in several illegal activities, including stolen cattle, counterfeit money and gambling, over the past ten years. (In fact, a member of the Thomas family remembered seeing Deere at a Thomas family home on at least one occasion.) Deere was described as a trader in cattle and other things but had no regular occupation. Some suspected that Deere was with Thomas in Littlefield, either on the Sunday before the Hunt murders, or both Sunday and Monday. At least two Littlefield citizens had seen two strangers in a car near the Hunt neighborhood prior to the murders.

About noon, Thomas and Deere were seen talking on Main Street in Durant. What happened from that point on comes only from Deere himself. He later told Police Chief Ben Risner that Thomas was angry and accused him of misrepresenting the condition of a two-ton 1950 Ford truck Deere had sold him. He said that Thomas also accused him of not returning an electric drill that Deere had borrowed and told him, "I'll give you just two hours to get that drill or I'll beat hell out of you."

Deere said he went home and loaded his double-barreled shotgun and leaned it up against a dining room wall. Shortly after noon, Thomas went to Deere's home at 626 West Evergreen Street and forced his way into the house. Deere said Thomas was still angry and slapped him in the face. Scared, Deere retrieved his shotgun from the dining room as Thomas approached. He said Thomas was only about two feet away when he fired both barrels. One load caught Thomas in the chest and the other in the lower abdomen. He died instantly, falling lengthwise in the doorway between the living and dining rooms.

After the shooting, Deere said he went out the back door and leaned the shotgun against the wall. He then walked to the fire station, where he called the funeral home to pick up the body and surrendered himself to Chief Risner, who was a distant relative. There were no witnesses to the shooting as Deere's wife and four children were visiting relatives in Amarillo. Bryan County sheriff Bob Barker stated that Thomas was not armed at the time; only a pocket knife was found on him.

The killing of fifty-six-year-old Jim Clyde Thomas was big news in the region. The *Durant Daily Democrat* ran a front-page photo of Thomas at the Gus Pool and Son Funeral Home. The headline of the *Oklahoman* read, "Texas Bad Man Forgets his Gun—Dies in Durant." The *Waco Times-Herald*, from Thomas's hometown, began the article with, "Jim Thomas at End of Trail," and the *Amarillo Daily News* ran the headline, "Jim Thomas Killed by Shotgun Blasts—Oklahoman Slays Gangster After Dispute Over Truck." The articles recounted the shooting and then touched on Thomas's thirty-four-year crime career, including the 1931 Hastings, Nebraska bank robbery and shootout.

Newspapers recounted Thomas's background, pointing out that he was suspected in the murders of Lon Holley and Que Miller, both found shot to death in their cars; the nitro blast of Nelson Harris and his pregnant wife; the bombing of Herbert Noble; and the Hunt murders.

Deere stated that he had known Jim Thomas for ten years and that they had considerable dealings together. "I know his record and know he was a dangerous man. I was scared when he threatened me and came to my house."

The Oklahoma State Crime Bureau records showed that Deere had numerous arrests but no convictions. Texas Rangers held him at Texarkana in 1942 for investigation, but there was no disposition.

County attorney R.H. Mills filed a murder charge against Deere, and a $5,000 bond was set. He was able to post bond thanks to friends who raised the money. Shortly after the hearing, Mills stated, "I think there was something far more important involved in the argument than an electric drill…I believe the whole thing goes deeper than most people have any idea." He went on to say that the 1950 Ford truck that Deere supposedly had sold to Thomas was seen by neighbors at the Deere home.

Even though Deere indicated no concern for an underworld reprisal for killing Thomas, Mills stated that he would discuss it with him. It was decided that Deere's family would remain in Amarillo for the time being.

Mary Thomas (nee Mary Burton, married 1945) went to Durant the next day to claim her husband's body, which was then sent to the Compton Funeral

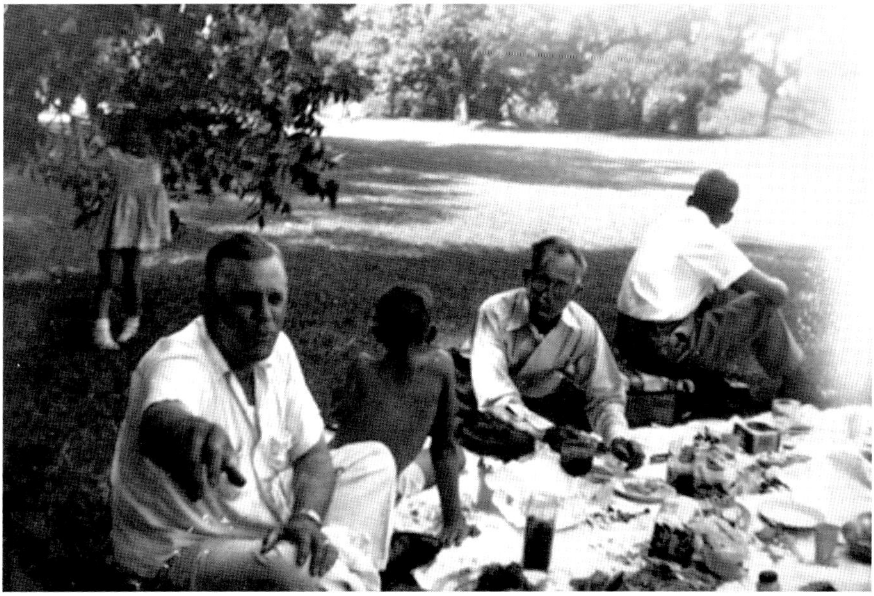

A rare snapshot of Jim Clyde Thomas (reaching toward camera) at a family picnic in the late 1940s. *Courtesy of Cyndi Snokhous.*

Home in Waco. She denied all contact with reporters and photographers. What she thought of her dead husband's photo on the front page of the Durant newspaper wasn't reported.

Three Fort Worth police detectives went to Durant to interview Deere. When asked by reporters for their reaction to the shooting, they described Jim Thomas as "one of the most cold-blooded trigger men" in the underworld. Other veteran officers said that despite his fancy clothes and swanky Fort Worth home, they regarded him as perhaps "the toughest of all the current crop of Texas toughs." It was said that "he was entirely cool and void of emotion under the most extreme circumstances." He was described as "a six-footer with silvery hair, a smooth line of talk and an expensive wardrobe, of which he was proud."

The detectives discussed the timing of Thomas's killing, coming only two weeks after Herbert Noble was killed. Sheriff Barker added that Deere had been charged with a misdemeanor bad check in Denton County involving the purchase of some machinery. Noble's ranch was located in Denton County. No one knew whether there was any connection. Deere added to his story; he claimed he had returned the electric drill, giving it to Thomas's associates in Midland, Texas. Investigators must have thought it was a bit peculiar for

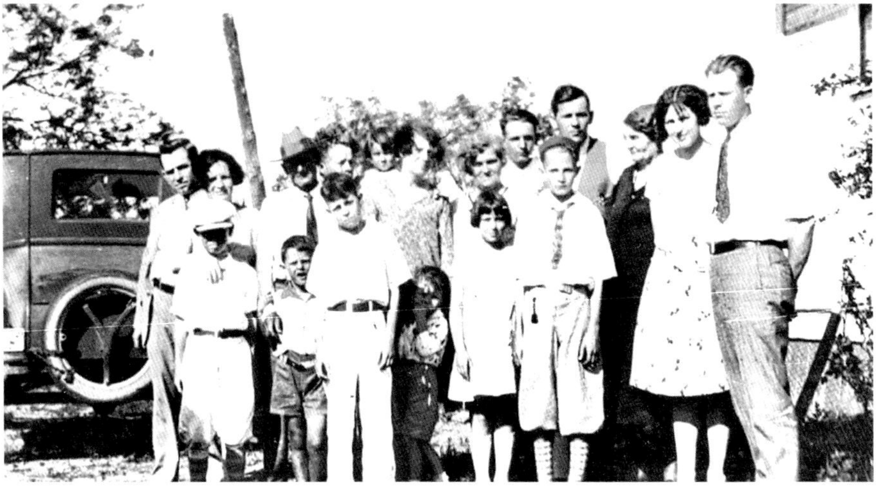

Family reunion, 1928. Jim Thomas is the tall, dark-haired man, fourth from the right. *Courtesy of Carl Montgomery.*

a man to drive 425 miles to return a drill, especially when Thomas lived in Fort Worth, only 122 miles from Deere's house. In yet another statement, he said that he told Thomas he had returned the drill to his Fort Worth home.

Further investigation uncovered phone calls between Jack Darby, "Big Boy" Burton (Thomas's father-in-law) and a man in Tucson, Arizona. Darby had been one of Herbert Noble's partners in his Dallas gambling enterprises. It was noted that Benny Binion had a contact in Tucson, but it wasn't known who received the call. A phone call was made from the Thomas home to Darby right after Thomas was killed. Why? Did Jim Clyde Thomas become too "hot" after the Noble hit, especially for Binion? It was known that Burton was not happy about his daughter's marriage to Thomas. In addition to Jim Clyde's reputation, there was also the fact that she was in her twenties and Thomas was in his fifties. Could that have been a reason for the killing? Years before, both Darby and Burton had worked in one of Binion's Fort Worth clubs.

The Forth Worth detectives showed Deere photos of Frank Cates and Jack Nesbit. He admitted to having seen the two men with Thomas in Oklahoma but denied having any business with them.

After the interview, Sheriff Barker said that he believed that Deere knew more than he was telling. "It doesn't seem likely that a man like Thomas would drive to Durant from Fort Worth to argue over an electric drill." He made it clear that he didn't believe Deere's story of the shooting and acknowledged that the truth might never be known. The sheriff told reporters he had heard within the last few months that some bootleggers around Durant had their loads hijacked. A man from the Fort Worth area was supposedly involved. The losses to the bootleggers were believed to be $6,000 to $7,000.

Hubert Deere pleaded innocent to killing Jim Thomas on the grounds of self-defense. His trial started on November 15, 1951. It ended after three hours of deliberation with a hung jury, six for and six against conviction, and a mistrial was declared. Obviously, half of the jury didn't believe Deere's story either. County Attorney Mills had contended during the trial that Thomas had been led into a trap. Sheriff Barker's words—"The truth may never be known"—rang true. A second trial never took place. In 1959, the case against Deere was dropped.

CHAPTER 15

Creighton and the '54 Missouri Penitentiary Riot

You old dog, your time has come.
—*William Hoover, as reported in the* Chillicothe Constitution-Tribune, *January 25, 1955*

In 1836, the same year that the Alamo fell to Santa Anna's forces in Texas, the Missouri State Penitentiary opened at Jefferson City. The one cellblock, a keeper's house and utility buildings were surrounded by a wall made of locally quarried stone. It was the first prison west of the Mississippi River. Jefferson City would eventually expand around the prison, which was located on a bank of the Missouri River.

In 1937, a dual-seated gas chamber was built. Thirty-eight murderers, rapists and kidnappers (including one female) were executed between 1938 and 1965. Double executions occurred four times.

During the prison's 168-year history (1836–2004), several infamous characters occupied its cells. Socialist-activist Kate Richards O'Hare and Russian-born anarchist Emma Goldman were convicted of interfering with military personnel recruitment under the Espionage Act of 1917. They were sent to the Missouri prison, which, at the time, was the only one that housed females. Midwest gangster Charles Arthur "Pretty Boy" Floyd called the prison home in 1925, as did 1962 world heavyweight champion Sonny Liston in 1950. In fact, Liston learned to box there. In 1959, Illinois native James Earl Ray was sentenced to twenty years in the Missouri penitentiary for robbery. He escaped on April 23, 1967, and became a household name

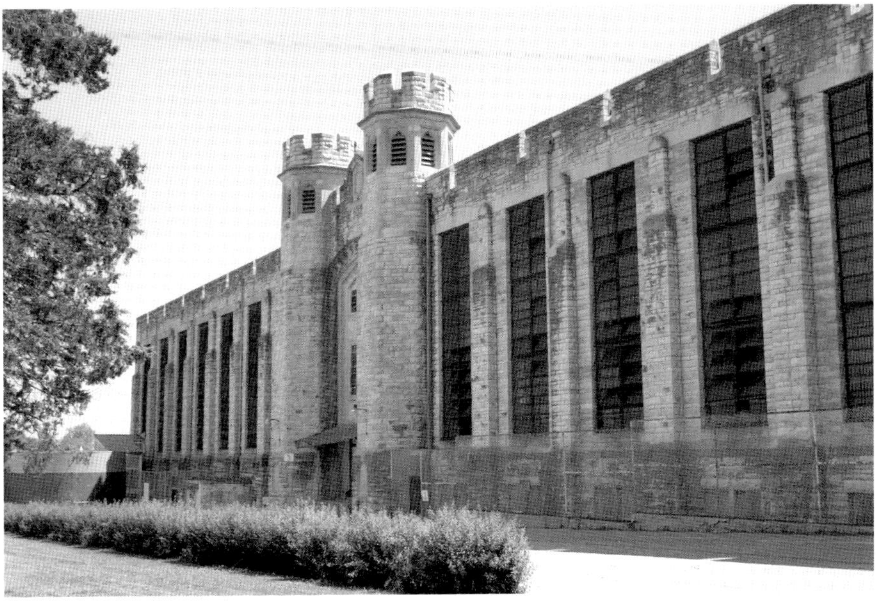

Building number 3 of the Missouri State Penitentiary. Death row was in the basement of this building. *Author's photo.*

the following year when he assassinated Dr. Martin Luther King Jr. in Memphis, Tennessee.

Hastings bank bandit and murderer Jimmy Creighton had been incarcerated in the Missouri State Penitentiary for thirteen years before his escape on July 8, 1944, from Prison Farm No. 2 (known as the Renz farm). In September 1945, he was arrested in Texas on a robbery charge and subsequently returned to the Missouri prison. At some point, Creighton had earned the reputation of a snitch and, for his protection, was housed on death row, "B" block, in the basement of Housing Unit 3. Walter Donnell, who had snitched on some St. Louis gang members, occupied the cell next to Creighton's.

On September 22, 1954, only two days after a powerful wind and rainstorm struck Jefferson City, prison sirens wailed. Inmates feigning illness overpowered guards, took their keys and opened cells. The inmates broke out windows and set buildings on fire. Jefferson City police responded, and Missouri State Highway Patrol troopers were summoned from across the state. Police from Kansas City and St. Louis were called in, along with Missouri National Guard troops. The prison housed 3,291 inmates, and over 2,000 were loose and out of control.

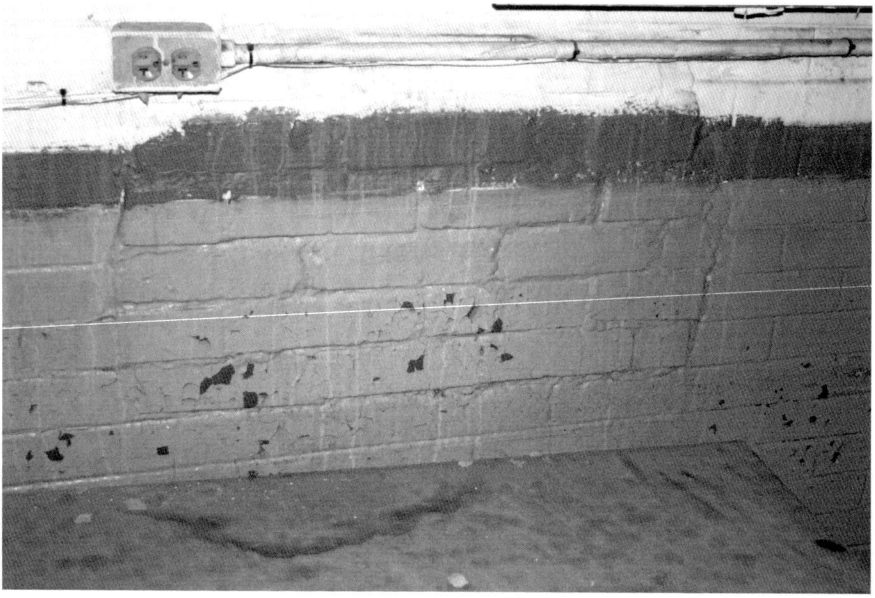

Rioting prisoners broke through this wall of a staff office to reach fellow inmates on death row. The author and wife discovered this previously unknown spot, which was repaired many years ago. *Courtesy of Ann McCord.*

During the riot, inmates made their way to death row, where they planned to free more inmates and take care of the two snitches housed there. Unable to open the main barred door, they entered the nearby office of Gail Hughes, a caseworker with Probation and Parole. Using a sledgehammer, they broke through the brick office wall and crawled through. After overpowering guard Clarence Dietzel, they were able to free inmates in death row's "B" block.

With sledgehammer, other tools and knives in hand, seven inmates went to the end of the block to Jimmy Creighton's cell and tried to force it open. William Hoover reportedly said to Creighton, "You old dog, your time has come." Creighton hurriedly jammed small pieces of concrete and other debris into the lock preventing it from being opened. He also used a piece of a chair to beat away his attackers. One of them had a broom and continually jabbed at Creighton with the wooden handle until finally hitting the mark, breaking his jaw.

Discouraged, they moved to Walter Donnell's cell and were successful in opening it. Creighton would later testify that he heard Donnell screaming, "I ain't no snitch!" The inmates stabbed Donnell with an ice

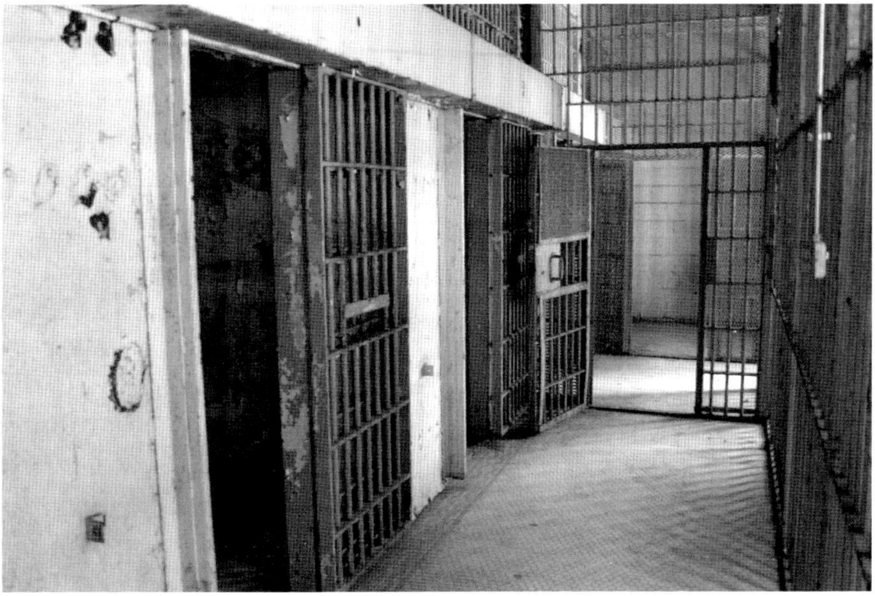

Building number 3, "B" block basement. These last cells on death row housed stool pigeons Walter Donnell and Jimmy Creighton. Donnell was murdered in his cell by rioting inmates. *Author's photo.*

pick and slashed at him with knives before one of the bunch finished the job with the sledgehammer.

Law enforcement officers were stationed around the outside of the prison with orders to "shoot to kill" any inmate who climbed over the wall. State troopers fired into the air and then at the rioters in an attempt to get them back inside the cell houses. A contingent of troopers then entered a cell house. They were met with threats and flying debris. The prisoners were ordered to get into the nearest cell or be shot. One shouting inmate apparently ignored the order and was shot dead. That seemed to achieve the desired affect. Inmates slowly filed into cells, some holding as many as nine men.

By the following morning, the still-smoking penitentiary was quiet. No escapes were made, but the damage done was estimated at the time to be $5 million. Fifty inmates were injured and four killed. Four guards were injured.

The cause of the riot would take a little time to sort out. Some believed that is was a ruse for inmates to kill the two snitches on death row. Some blamed bad food and living conditions over a period of time. It became apparent that the inmates were also protesting the makeup of the prison administration and parole board, positions held by former state troopers.

Jimmy Creighton agreed to testify against the seven inmates who were accused of killing Walter Donnell and was moved to the Cole County jail. He may have been promised something for his testimony. During the seven trials throughout the following year, he would be asked about that amid accusations that he was allowed extra perks in the county jail, including access to female inmates. The fact that Creighton had been treated at the Fulton State Mental Hospital for thirty days the previous spring was also revealed. The six inmates accused in the killing—Don DeLapp, William Hoover, Jack Noble, Rollie Laster, Paul Kenton and James Stidham—were all found guilty.

James Marvin Creighton was granted a commutation of his life sentence and walked out of the Cole County jail on January 13, 1956. County prosecutor James T. Riley told the news media at the end of January that he had approached Governor Phil Donelly to commute the sentence, saying, "We had to do something with Creighton, we couldn't take him back out to the prison." Of course they knew that Creighton, now a *major* stool pigeon, couldn't be protected if sent back to prison. Interestingly, the chairman of the parole board said that normally prison records of commutation applicants are checked, but he didn't remember any check of Creighton's record by his staff.

Upon his release, Creighton was told that he'd have to protect himself from then on. Free only a few days, he was stopped by police in Oklahoma and released after Missouri replied that they had no hold on him.

The story of the 1954 prison riot did not end there, however. The convicted inmates would file appeals, some running into the 1970s. The inmates continued their claims of being beaten and tortured by troopers and policemen for their admissions of guilt. They also said that they offered to take polygraph tests but were denied the opportunity. It was rumored that the real perpetrators in Donnell's murder were St. Louis inmates.

On May 30, 1975, a story outlining the prison riot murder case ran on page one of the *Kansas City Star*. The reporter was J.J. Maloney, an ex-convict himself, who had spent three and a half years in reform schools and thirteen years in prison for an armed robbery and murder he had committed at age nineteen. He was also an award winning author/journalist who garnered five Pulitzer Prize nominations for his articles. Maloney's article, "In the Wake of a Riot," was an exposé of the riot and prosecutions. He found that renowned St. Louis trial lawyer Mark Henelly had taken up the cases of the convicted inmates following the indictments and had continued to work on their behalf into the 1970s. Henelly was an attorney (later president) for the Missouri Pacific Railroad.

The polygraph is not admissible in court but is a very good investigative tool. In the early 1970s, Maloney found ex–Missouri trooper Carroll Price at a college in Kansas City where he taught polygraph testing. Price had been on duty at the prison during the riot and, strangely, would have been the one tasked with administering polygraph tests to the six inmates, had they been allowed to take them. The *Kansas City Star* agreed to sponsor a polygraph test given by Price to James Stidham at the prison. Maloney reported that he passed the test. Maloney tracked down several of the troopers and St. Louis policemen who had conducted the interrogations of the seven inmates. None would talk to him.

Maloney's article mentioned witness James Creighton several times, including a story that since being imprisoned he had murdered another inmate by throwing gasoline into his cell. Creighton had also slashed the throat of another inmate. The newspaper article stated, "Creighton was dead" (by 1975), but didn't elaborate. The contact with Oklahoma authorities in 1956 was the last ever heard of Jimmy Creighton. It's unknown where, when or how he died.

Some of the infamous six inmates died in prison, and others finally won parole but were returned for various violations. A few were able stay out of prison and live out their lives. Mark Henelly died in 1983 after fighting a twenty-nine-year legal battle for Stidham.

A second riot broke out at the prison only a month after the September conflagration. It seemed to be based on food quality and resulted in the death of one inmate and injury to thirty-nine others. The riots did finally bring about major prison reform on many levels in the state of Missouri.

CHAPTER 16

A Copper Reunion

He sprayed the whole backyard!
—Thomas Dryden, as reported in the Hastings Tribune, *May 31, 1983*

In 1979, the author interviewed former Hastings policeman Tommy Dryden in Omaha, Nebraska. Dryden was eighty years old at the time, and it appeared only wrinkles had changed him, his Brooklyn accent still strong. He answered most questions about his police experiences as if they had happened yesterday. Of course, a man firing a Thompson submachine gun in your direction would surely stick in anyone's mind.

Thomas "Tommy" James Dryden was born in Brooklyn, New York, on July 2, 1899. He came to Adams County, Nebraska, in 1918. A conversation at a Hastings gas station in 1929 prompted him to look into police work. George Harms and Charles Ingraham had remarked in Dryden's presence, "Tommy would make a good motorcycle man." Dryden applied for the job and was hired by the Hastings police in April of that year.

Dryden explained that he reported to the police station located on the second floor of a dry goods store at First Street and Hastings Avenue. Bob Carter was chief. Soon thereafter, John Bramble took over the chief's job. The new chief directed all new officers to have their portraits taken at Stephens Studio. Dryden made $125 a month until the Depression set in, when wages were reduced to $80.

On one occasion, Dryden was in the chief's office where a salesman was showing a new bulletproof vest that he wore. The salesman took Dryden's

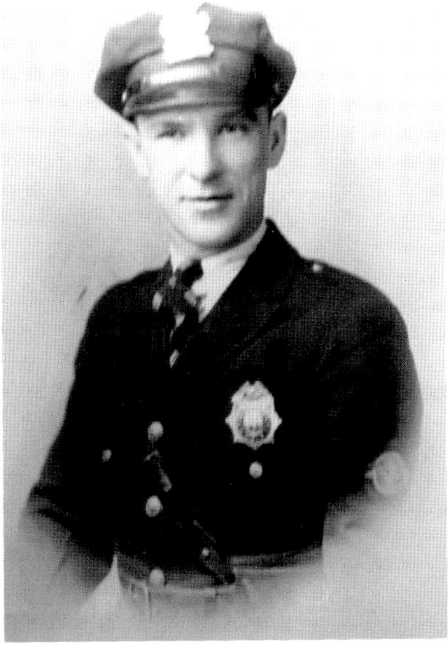

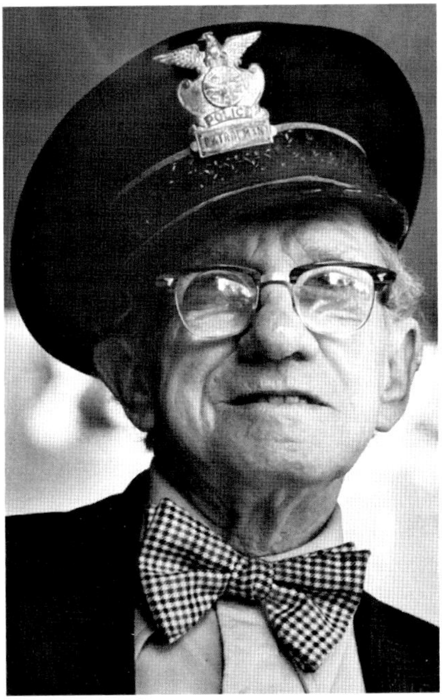

Above, left: Portrait of Patrolman Tommy Dryden taken at Stephens Studio when he joined the Hastings police department in 1929. *Author's collection.*

Above, right: Tommy Dryden at the author's home for a 1983 reunion with Ray Thomas. He is wearing a Hastings police hat from the 1930s. *Courtesy of the* Hastings Tribune.

.38 revolver, turned the gun on himself and fired. Dryden said, "I thought he was a damned fool!"

He reminisced about the day of the Hastings National Bank robbery and being one of the eight officers who went to the East Sixth Street house. Dryden and Volcott Condit took up a position at the back door. "I was looking through this back glass door, but I couldn't see the guys." He then saw one of the bandits coming down stairs leading to the back door. "I was gonna surprise him, so I cocked back my gun." Instead the bandit surprised him by shooting through the back door with a machine gun. "He sprayed the whole backyard!"

A couple years after the interview with Dryden, the author located another policeman, Ray Thomas, who worked in 1931. After the shooting started at the bandit house, help was called. Responding were Chief Bramble, Sheriff Crosson, Captain Yetman and Night Sergeant Ray Thomas. Thomas's experience at the shootout didn't last long, as the police surrendered under the barrel of the machine gun shortly after arrival.

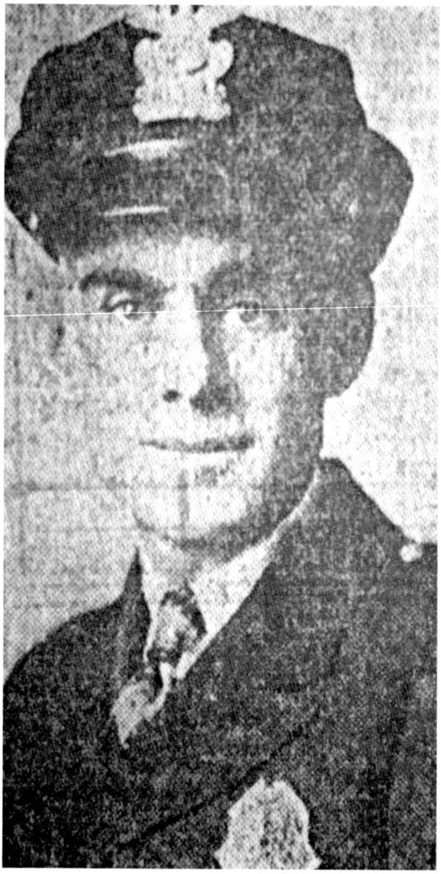

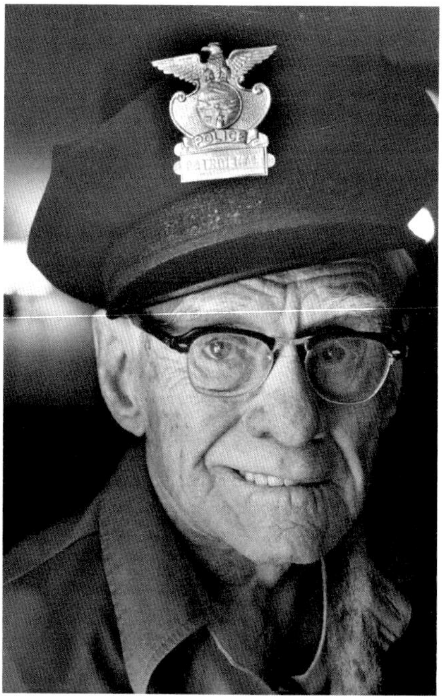

Left: Hastings patrolman Ray Thomas in 1931. *Courtesy of the* Hastings Tribune.

Above: Ray Thomas in 1983, at the author's home. *Courtesy of the* Hastings Tribune.

In May 1983, the author arranged for a reunion of the two policemen. Dryden was eighty-three years old, and Thomas was ninety. The two oldest living Hastings policemen hadn't seen each other in fifty years.

Thomas said that he took the police job for its regular hours and good pay, important in the hard times of the 1930s. When asked if he had been scared by the dangers of police work, he replied, "I never gave it much thought."

A *Hastings Tribune* reporter took photos of Dryden and Thomas wearing authentic Hastings police hats from the early 1930s. Ironically, a photo ran in the same newspaper around Christmastime of 1930 featuring Hastings city officials. Included in the photo were Chief Bramble and two uniformed officers—Tommy Dryden and Ray Thomas.

Tommy Dryden resigned from the police department in 1934 to run for Adams County sheriff but was defeated by Worthy Wood. His wife died the

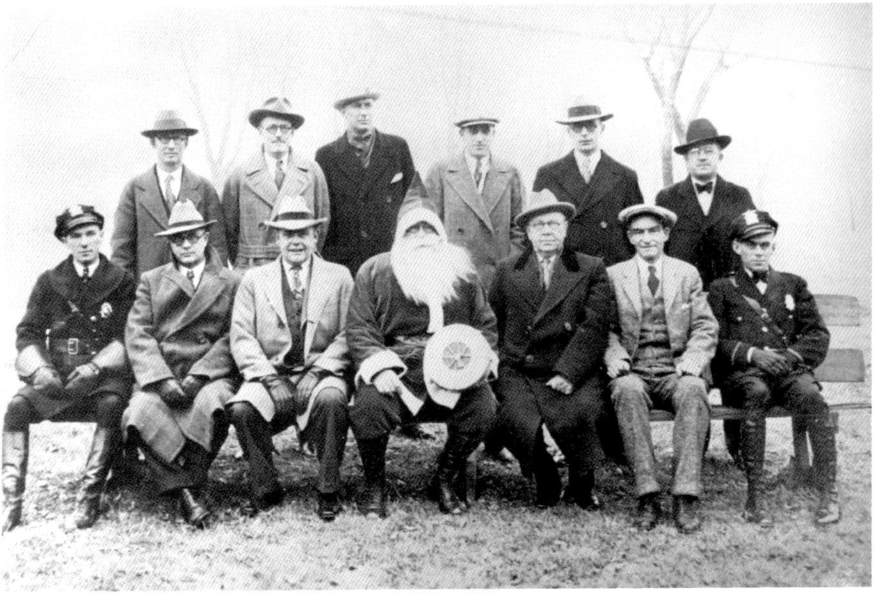

Hastings city officials, December 1930. Tallest man in back row is Police Chief John Bramble. Patrolman Tommy Dryden is at far left and Patrolman Ray Thomas at far right. Mayor Joe Davis is next to Santa Claus in light coat. *Courtesy of the* Hastings Tribune.

same year. Dryden then held a position with the city fire department for a year. He left Hastings in the 1940s.

Ray Thomas ran a café from 1932 until 1950, when he became a salesman for the Farmers Mutual Insurance Company. He served as an Adams County deputy sheriff and tax collector from 1957 until his retirement in 1962.

Thomas passed away only two years after the reunion, and Dryden lived another six years.

Afterword

The Hastings bank robbery of 1931 was talked about for years. Even though the incident, at times, seemed more like an episode of the *Keystone Kops*, some realized the real danger bank officials and police had been in. If those people had known what the bandits would do later on, they would have truly realized that, for a time, lives *did* hang in the balance. Things had gone wrong during some of the other Midwest bank robberies; lives had been lost, and families changed forever.

As I studied this bank robbery, it was interesting to see how many opportunities there were for the bandits' discovery. The clothes left by Lonnie Mills inside the house before the "Hendrickses" rented it was a start. The strange hours the men kept and their demeanor while doing business around town were suspicious. Giving a second alias at the Chevrolet garage when Thomas had the car worked on and paying a laundry charge with a fifty-dollar bill during the Depression were certainly suspect. Their interactions with the coal delivery man and the paperboy at the house seemed unnecessary. But their demeanor at the house would be what helped to discover them. Hastings police had actually been checking out the house before the robbery. Officers testified later that they suspected them of being bootleggers.

Establishing the identity of the four bandits (which actually turned into five) and Velma Creighton was not as easy as initially thought. Though he denied it, Lonnie Mills had come to Hastings as a scout and had located the rental house on the east edge of town. Chief Bramble noted the size difference in Mills's clothes and Jimmy Creighton, thereby discrediting his claim of trading a suit with Creighton. Mills also admitted knowing and being in business with Jim Thomas and the others.

This gang robbed the Canyon, Texas bank about two weeks before coming to Hastings. Unluckily for Mills, he was the only one nabbed on February 6 and was not released until after the Hastings job. His arrest necessitated that Thomas and Creighton find a replacement man. The Sunday before the robbery, Thomas and Creighton visited Virgil Johnson's home near Longdale, Oklahoma (where Creighton had been staying). They enlisted Johnson. The day after the Hastings bank job, Creighton and Johnson returned to the Johnson home, hurriedly sold their furniture to Bobbie Cubic and left. Johnson's wife paid off bills in town with gold before she and her sister left for Tulsa. Creighton later bought a new car, and the two (Creighton and Johnson) paid a gas station operator south of Tulsa in gold. There they met up with Johnson's wife and sister.

In his 1940 pardon board hearing, Thomas told the board a partial truth; Mills had "backed out" (so to speak), so Creighton went to Oklahoma and brought back a man who Thomas claimed he knew only as "Bill." Thomas was actually with Creighton when they went to Oklahoma to pick him up and most assuredly knew "Bill" was actually Virgil Johnson. As William Condit explained, "Men like that wouldn't go into a bold robbery like this without knowing exactly who was with them." Creighton said as much in an interview with Condit.

It's difficult to know for sure which one of the four men stayed with the car outside the Hastings National Bank that morning as driver and lookout. But Mr. Cox would later confirm there was a man in a car as he walked by to check the bank thermometer shortly after 6:00 a.m. Harry Marian would also state that he saw the car drive west down Third Street at a fast rate, not stopping for a signal, and he believed there were four men inside. They may have let out one of the gang before returning to the East Sixth Street house.

It will never be known who cut the outside window screen at the Adams County jail during the night of May 8 and passed a file and cash to Jim Thomas, helping him to escape. About the only member of the gang who could be ruled out was Velma Creighton. She was in Seminole, Oklahoma, awaiting the birth of her second child, which came late in May. The whereabouts of Jimmy Creighton (he had not yet committed murder in Missouri), Virgil Johnson, Lonnie Mills or, for that matter, Thomas's wife, Adelle, were unknown. Oddly, after his recapture, Thomas told reporters, "I had just as well say it was the third man in the bank job that helped me, because that's what the boys upstairs will think anyway. But it wasn't him, and I'm not saying who it was." An interesting side note to this was the letter from Texas that Sheriff Crosson received in which the gang threatened to break Thomas out of jail. Maybe this wasn't completely an idle threat, but they decided on the less noticeable mission of giving Thomas a file and cash.

We know fifty-six-year-old bandit leader James Thomas was shot and killed on August 22, 1951, and buried in Waco, Texas. Both the sheriff and county attorney felt the circumstances of his murder were suspicious and did not believe Hubert Deere's story.

Lonnie C. Mills had lived in Pampa, Texas, but moved to Oklahoma City in 1936. He was listed as an oil field worker. He died on August 19, 1936, of injuries sustained in an automobile accident. The thirty-seven-year-old Mills lingered three weeks before passing away. The death certificate listed the cause of death as bronchial asthma, fractured right femur and other injuries. He was buried in Seminole, Oklahoma.

Jimmy Creighton was released from the Missouri State Penitentiary in January 1956. By then a major stool pigeon, he had much to worry about. The inmates that he helped to convict in the Walter Donnell murder during the prison riot no doubt had friends on the outside. Nothing more was heard of Creighton after 1956. *Kansas City Star* reporter J.J. Maloney reported in 1975 that Creighton was dead, so he must have died sometime between 1956 and 1975.

Samuel Lawson O'Dell was released from the Montana State Prison on February 19, 1938, and turned over to U.S. Marshals to face Dyer Act charges.

As for Virgil Johnson, on December 20, 1934, Joplin, Missouri police received a report of two suspicious men in a car. Detectives Vandeventer and Caylor (the same detectives who arrested Jimmy Creighton in Joplin) responded to check them out. They ended up arresting Earl Maze, thirty-three, and H.G. Boyer, twenty-five, both of Rogers, Arkansas. Both suspects had automatic pistols on them, and Maze had three hacksaw blades hidden in his trousers. Also found in the car were rubber gloves, burglar tools, extra license plates, a loaded sawed-off shotgun and a quantity of ammunition.

The U.S. Division of Investigation identified Haze as Virgil Johnson, "a man widely sought in the $17,000 (*sic*) robbery of a Hastings, Neb., bank on February 25, 1931, and a former pal of James Creighton, convicted killer." The Division also indicated that Johnson had a criminal record dating back to 1919, when he was sent to the Oklahoma reformatory for grand larceny and had been implicated with Creighton in several Oklahoma and Kansas bank robberies.

Johnson told the detectives that he had bought a small fruit farm near Rogers, Arkansas, and was making payments on it. He admitted that he'd served a term in the Kansas State Penitentiary at Lansing for burglary and one for liquor violations but insisted that he "was going straight ever since." He also admitted that one of the pistols was his but wouldn't comment on why they were carrying all of the weapons in the car. At first he denied knowing Creighton but later admitted that he knew him. Of course, he denied being involved in any crimes with Creighton.

Joplin police notified Hastings about his arrest, but the *Lincoln Star* reported that there was little interest shown by authorities there. County attorney Herman Schroeder was in Omaha at the time, and Sheriff Crosson stated that Johnson would likely be able to come up with an alibi for the time of the bank robbery. Crosson added that it might be difficult to identify Johnson. William Condit, by that time Lincoln police chief, was quoted as saying he would attempt to get photos of Johnson and forward them to Hastings for identification. But it was obvious that after three years had passed, the interest in pursuing the case further was just not there. Crosson was probably correct, however, about witnesses not being able to identify Johnson.

Johnson was wanted along with Thomas, Creighton and Mills for the Canyon, Texas bank robbery as well, but the sheriff in Texas was unable to obtain extradition papers so the matter was dropped.

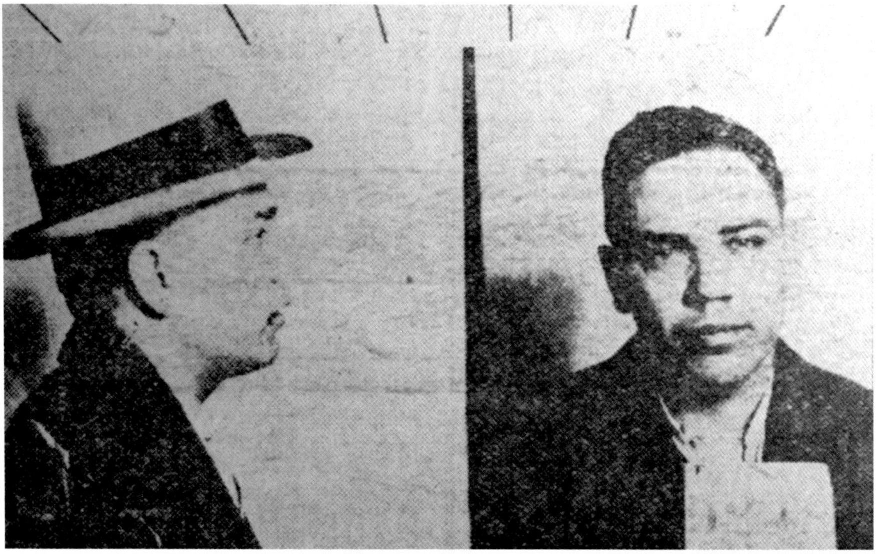

One of several mug shots furnished by the Burns detective agency, listed as "Clyde Nemerick," an alias believed to have been used by Lonnie Mills. As aliases were sometimes hard to keep straight, this man could quite possibly be Virgil Johnson. *Courtesy of the* Hastings Tribune.

Johnson ended up with a thirty-day sentence and fifty-dollar fine for carrying a concealed weapon. His wife and four-year-old daughter visited him in jail.

On June 3, 1936, Virgil Johnson and his brother Vernon were arrested after Vernon, drunk, attacked a man at the Aero Buffet in Joplin. It was unknown why he began beating W.A. Harbison on the head, but Harbison was found dead at the scene. Virgil was released after witnesses said it was only Vernon who attacked the man.

Velma Creighton filed for divorce in 1934, five months after Jimmy gouged his eyes at the Missouri penitentiary. She filed in Arkansas, one of three states known at the time for quick divorces. She later married a man who owned an oil lease in Oklahoma.

John Fredrick Bramble was born on April 16, 1892, and was thirty-eight years old when he became the Hastings police chief. He must have liked what he saw of Oklahoma during the manhunt as he and his wife, Jennie, eventually moved there to go into business. He died on March 16, 1964, and is buried in Oklahoma City.

James Lawrence Wood, the hostage officer tied to a telephone pole west of Grafton, Nebraska, along Highway 38, became Minden's chief of police shortly after the Hastings robbery.

Herman Schroeder was born in Elwood, Nebraska, in 1898. He served two terms as police magistrate and was the Adams County attorney from 1930 to 1934. A 1921 graduate of the University of Nebraska law school, Schroeder was a partner with John W. James until James was appointed district court judge. From then on, Schroeder carried on the practice alone. He was a member of many civic groups and had been president of the chamber of commerce. Suffering from "inflammatory heart disease" since the age of eight, he passed away at his home on March 26, 1937, at age thirty-eight. Schroeder was president of the Mary Lanning Memorial Hospital board of directors at the time of his death. Many mourned the passing of the well liked and respected citizen.

Yet some aspects of this story continue to defy discovery.

APPENDIX

Places and Tombstones

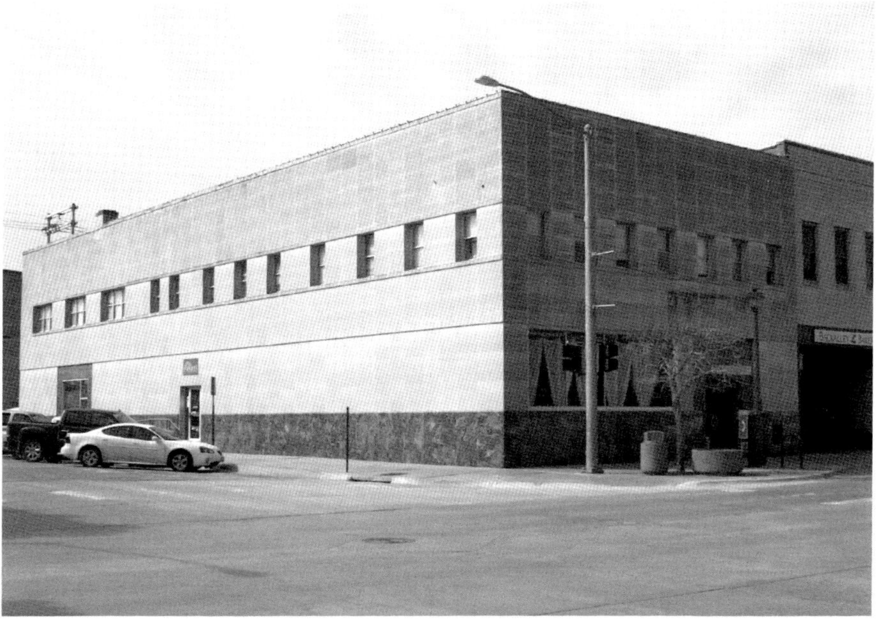

The Hastings National Bank building today. It was built in 1881 and has housed several different banks and businesses over the years. It currently houses two businesses. *Author's photo.*

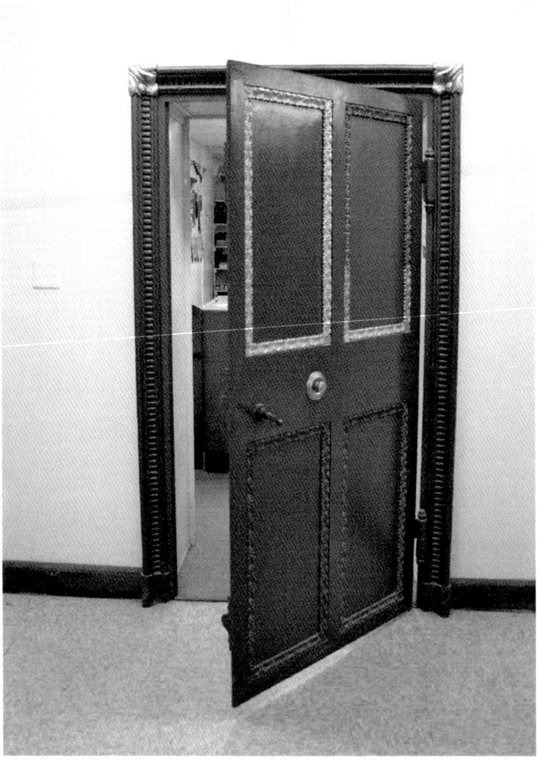

Left: The vault of the old bank building where the bandits removed over $27,000 in February 1931. The Coin Center now resides in the vault. The large, time lock vault door was removed many years ago. *Author's photo.*

Below: The bandits' house at 810 East Sixth Street as it appears today. It is still a rental. *Author's photo.*

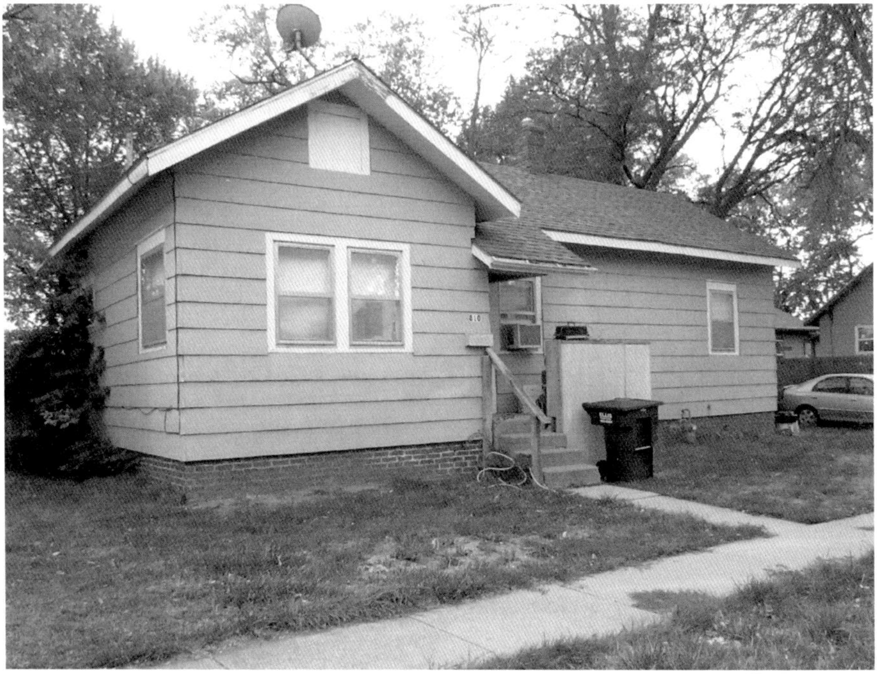

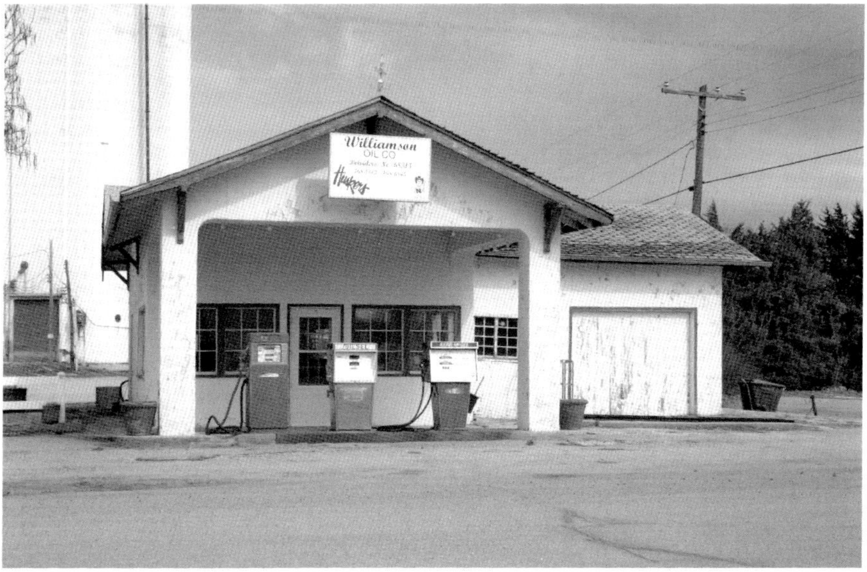

Belvidere, Nebraska filling station today. *Author's photo.*

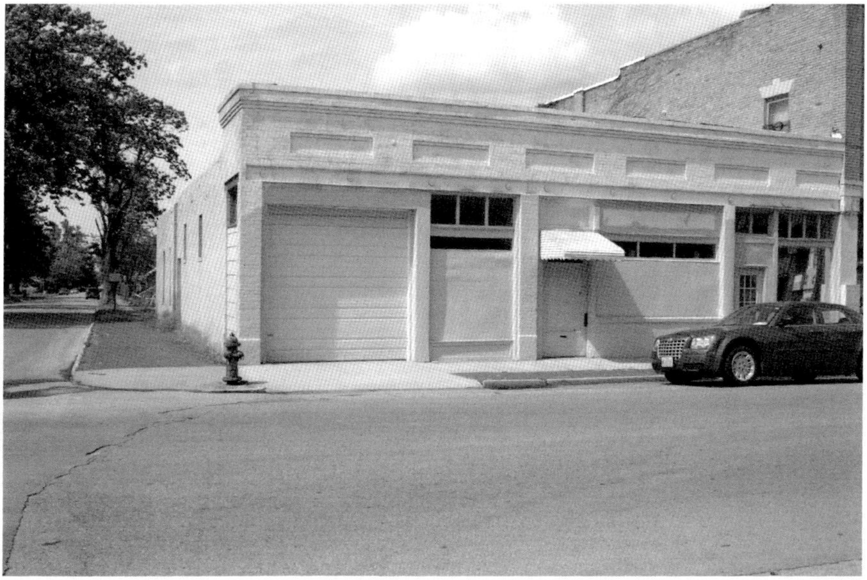

The Morgan Drug Co. store, Webb City, Missouri, today. *Author's photo.*

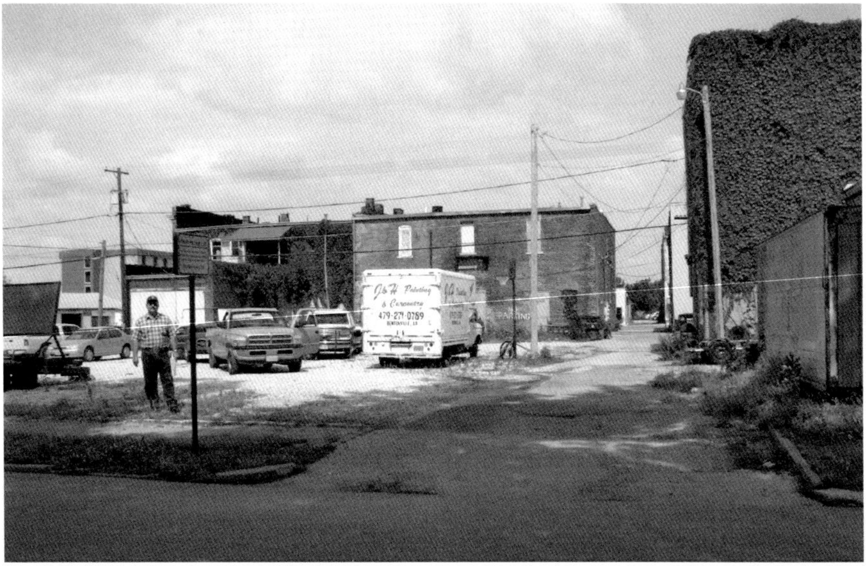

Modern view of the Coyne Hatten murder site behind the old Morgan Drug Co. store. *Author's photo.*

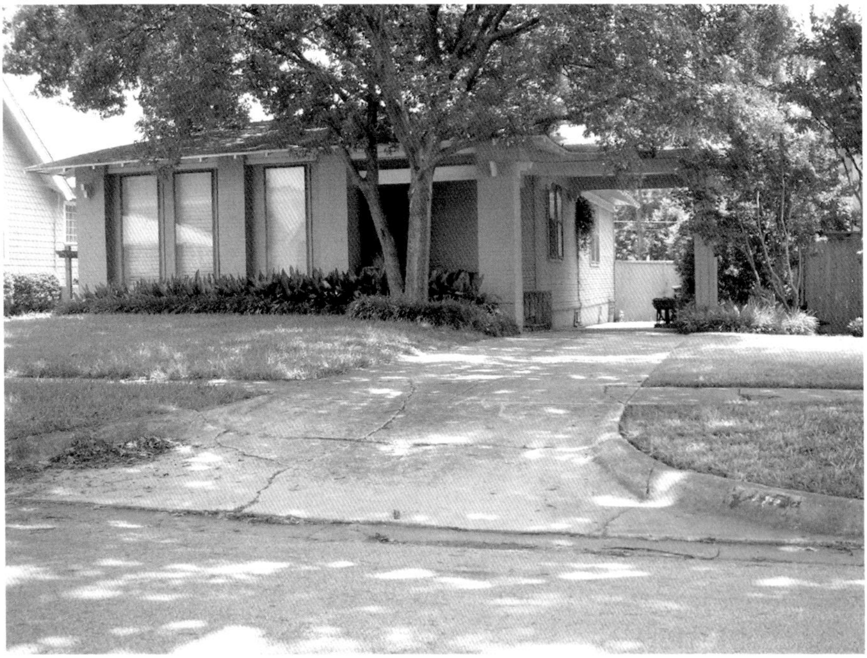

Jim Clyde Thomas's Fort Worth home today. *Courtesy of George Goldthwaite.*

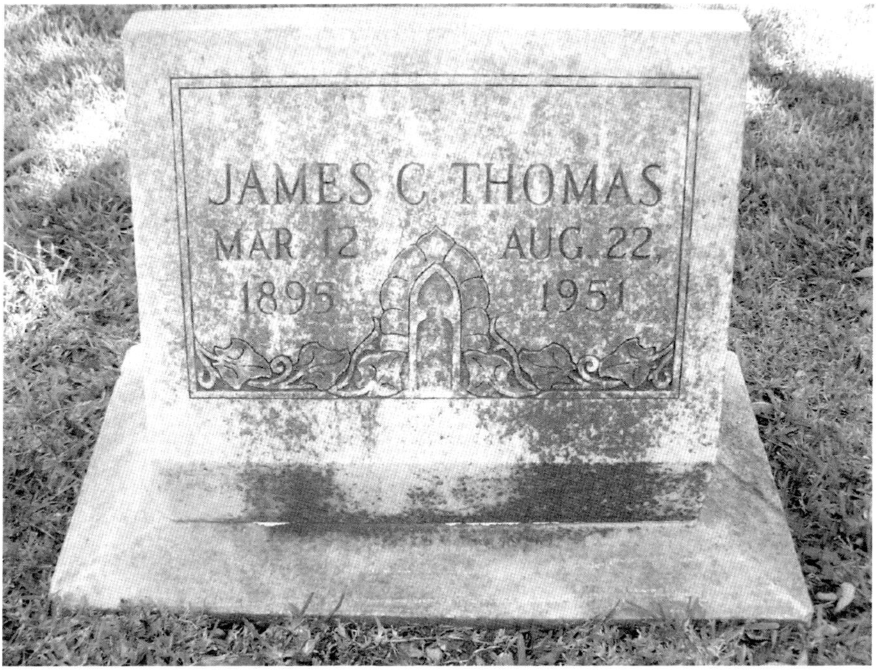

Jim Thomas, Oakwood Cemetery, Waco, Texas. *Courtesy of Peggy Duty, Central Texas Genealogical Society.*

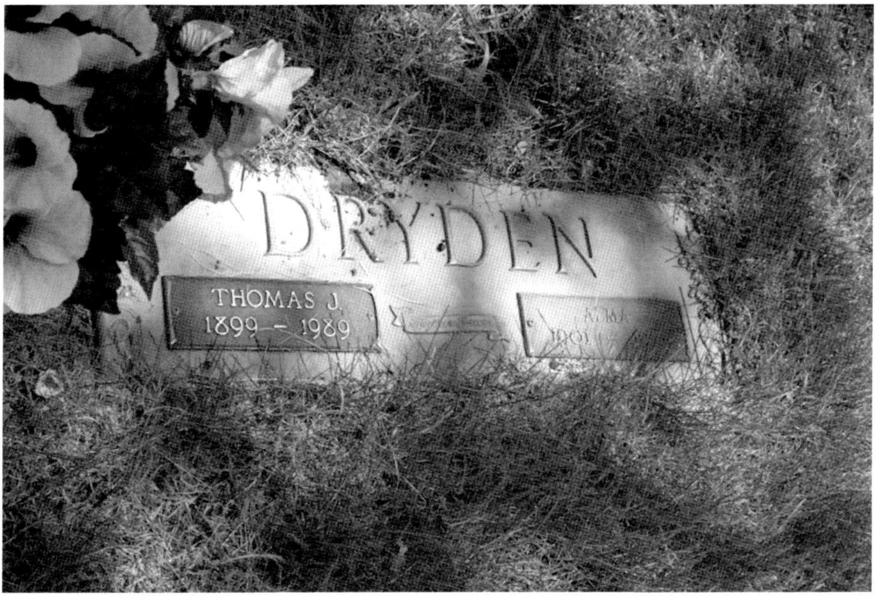

Tommy Dryden at Forest Lawn Memorial Park, Omaha, Nebraska. *Courtesy of Charlie Vogel.*

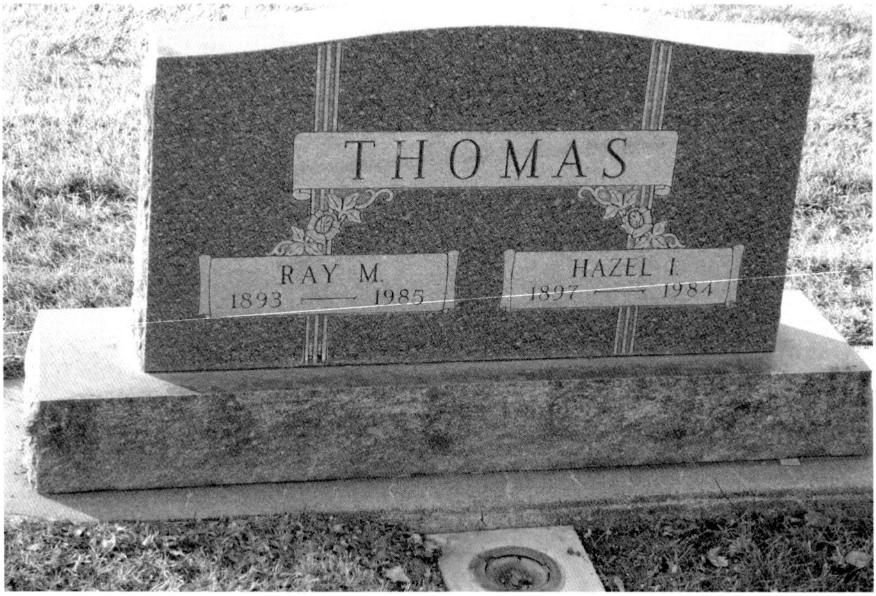

Ray Thomas, Parkview Cemetery, Hastings, Nebraska. *Author's photo.*

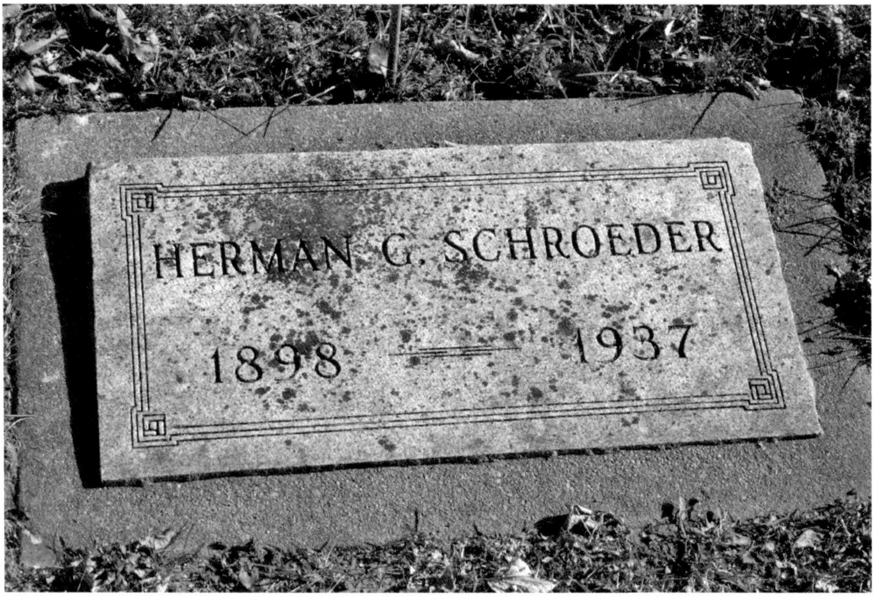

Herman Schroeder, Parkview Cemetery, Hastings, Nebraska. *Author's photo.*

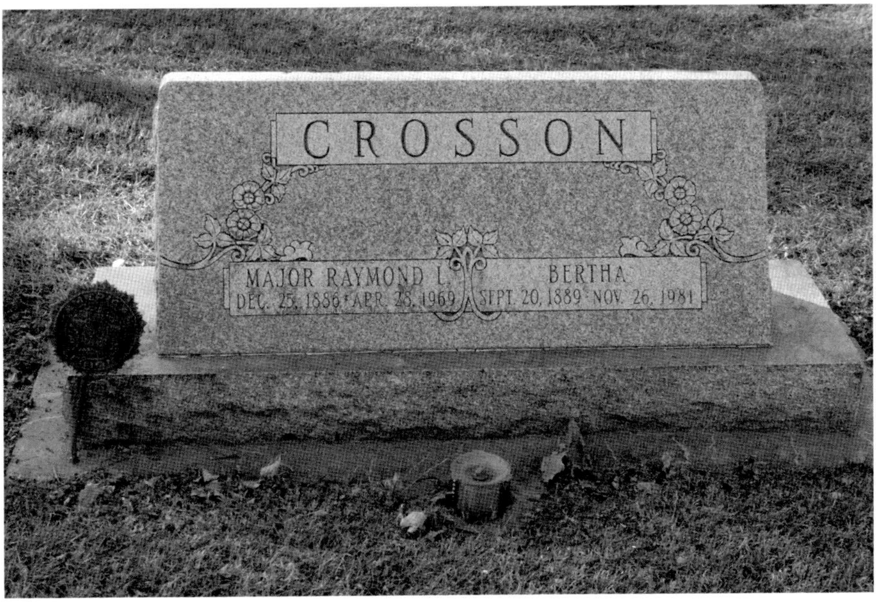

Ray Crosson, Parkview Cemetery, Hastings, Nebraska. *Author's photo.*

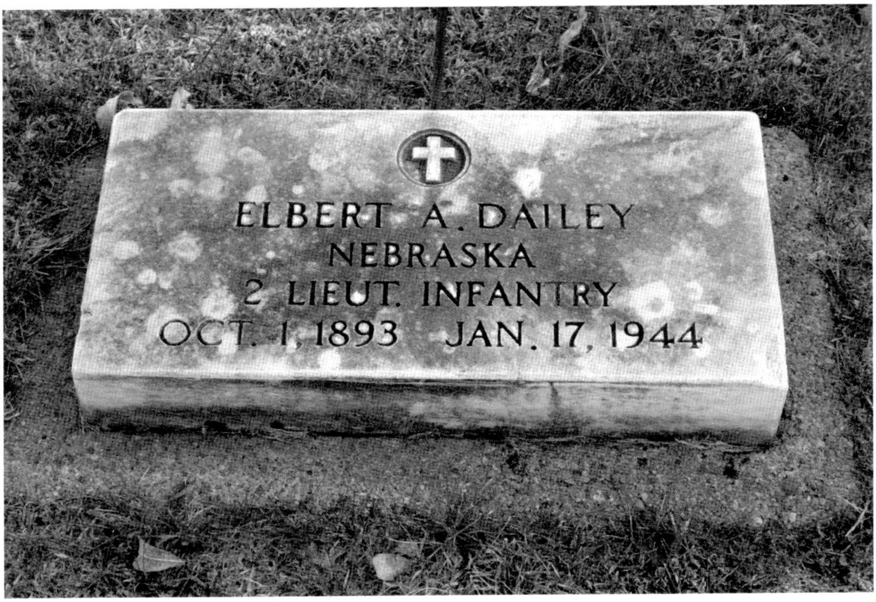

Elbert Dailey, Blue Valley Cemetery, Adams County, Nebraska. *Author's photo.*

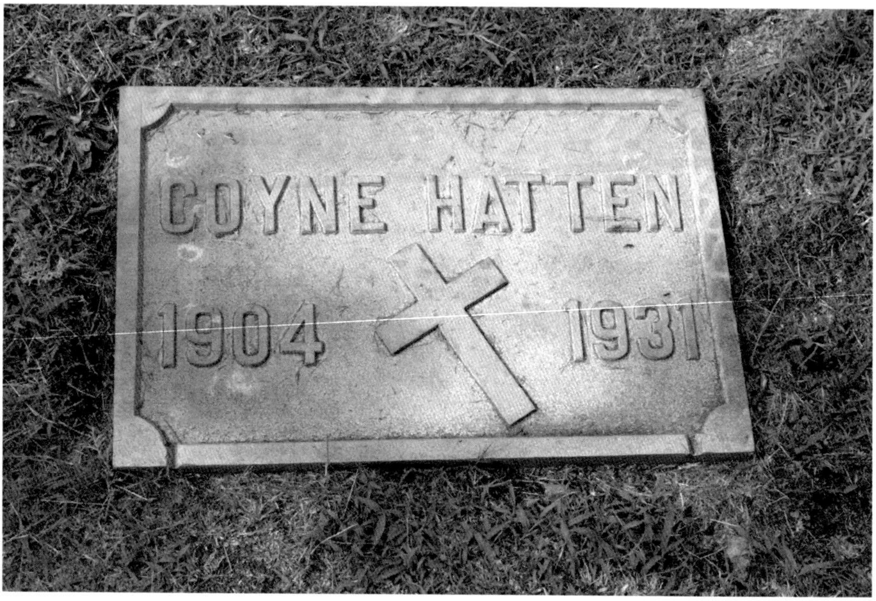

Coyne Hatten, Mount Hope Cemetery, Webb City, Missouri. *Author's photo.*

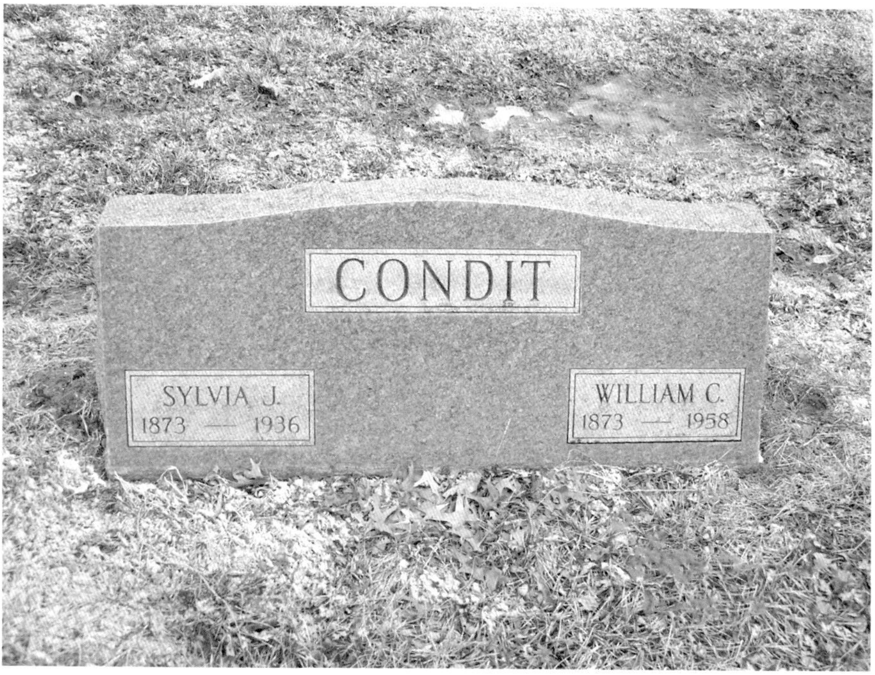

William Condit, Ridge Cemetery, Fremont, Nebraska. *Courtesy of Pat Toscano.*

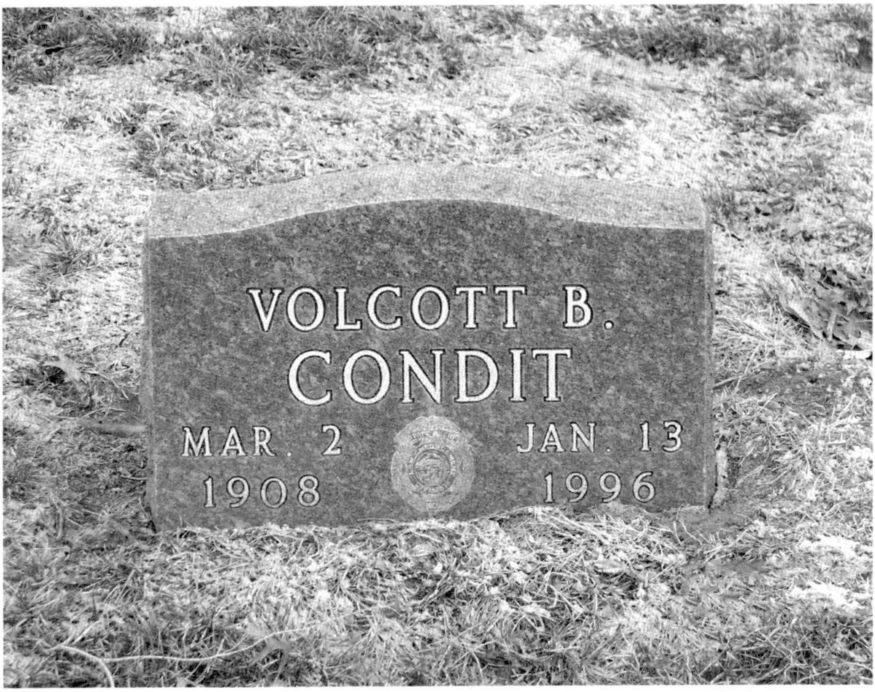

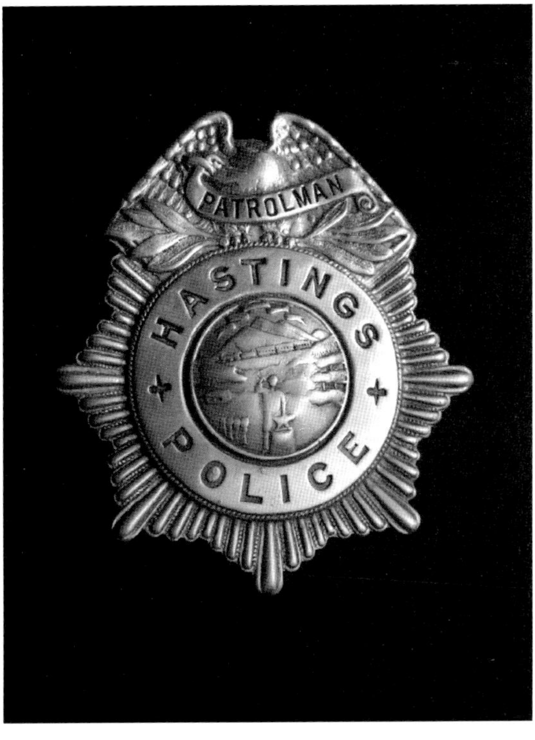

Above: Volcott Condit, Ridge Cemetery, Fremont, Nebraska. *Courtesy of Pat Toscano.*

Right: Badge used by Hastings police in 1930s. *Author's photo.*